ONE POT MEALS

ONE POT MEALS

MARGARET GIN

DRAWINGS BY RIK OLSON

101 PRODUCTIONS
SAN FRANCISCO

Printed and bound in the United States of America

Distributed to the book trade in the United States
by Charles Scribner's Sons, New York, and in Canada
by Van Nostrand Reinhold Ltd., Toronto

Published by 101 Productions
834 Mission Street
San Francisco, California 94103

Library of Congress Cataloging in Publication Data

Gin, Margaret.
    One pot meals.

    Includes index.
    1. Casserole cookery.   I. Title.
TX 693.G56   641.8'21   76-41173
ISBN O-89286-101-0
ISBN O-89286-100-2 pbk.

CONTENTS

A PRIMER OF POTS

One-pot cookery conserves time, fuel and fuss, while often preserving the flavor and nutritional value of foods. The tradition of one-pot cooking is probably as old as man's first efforts to cook his food and embraces most of the world's cuisines.

The Japanese cherish their "nabemono" dishes, which are one-pot meals cooked at the table over an hibachi and include the popular sukiyaki and shabu shabu. Over the centuries the Chinese, in an effort to conserve fuel, have developed the stir-fry method of wok cooking to a fine art.

Many one-pot dishes of Western Europe are culinary classics, identified as the hallmarks of each national cuisine—the paella of Spain, pot-au-feu and bouillabaisse of France, the hochepot of Belgium and the gilvetch of Romania.

In Colonial North America, one-pot cooking was symbolized by the Dutch oven hanging over the hearth. This cast-iron vessel of many purposes was later carried west by the American pioneers and even today, in its many streamlined forms, the Dutch oven is indispensable to most cooks.

Twentieth-century technology has made two significant contributions to preparing meals in a single pot: the pressure cooker, so popular during World War II, and the recently developed slow cooker, versions of which are now produced by some 30 manufacturers.

This book offers one-pot recipes from many countries, prepared in a number of ways. Where practical, several preparation methods have been listed for the same dish, i.e., a hearty stew may be cooked on top of the stove in a Dutch oven, in a pressure cooker, in a slow cooker or in a wet clay cooker. In most recipes, a skillet is interchangeable with a wok. Exotic cookware like fondue pots, chafing dishes, omelet pans and soufflé dishes can give variety to one-pot cookery, and recipes are given for their use. But even more useful are the commonplace basics of the *batterie de cuisine:* the all-purpose casserole, soup pot and roasting pan.

7

A PRIMER OF POTS

THE PRESSURE COOKER

Treasured by World War II homemakers as an indispensable aid to canning, the pressure cooker still has a place in the modern kitchen not only because home canning has experienced a revival, but because busy people everywhere have rediscovered this pot's versatility. The pressure cooker, like its offspring, the slow cooker, is a time-and-money saver. Because steam penetrates the food quickly, it reduces cooking time while retaining valuable vitamins and minerals.

The old-fashioned pressure cooker sat right on top of the stove. Newer electric models come with thermostatic heat controls. In all cases you should carefully follow the manufacturer's instructions for use and care. There are, however, a few basic rules for pressure cookers which apply to all models.

Do not overload the pressure cooker. When cooking soups or other liquids, the cooker should be filled to no more than half capacity. Two-thirds full is the rule of thumb for liquids combined with solids, like stews.

Reduce recipes for conventional cooking to one-fourth the time for the pressure cooker, not one-third as mentioned in many cookbooks. The cooking may always be finished not under pressure. With a stew, for example, the meat should be cooked under pressure, then the vegetables may be added and cooked after the pressure has been reduced. This preserves their flavor and freshness.

When using a pressure cooker, adjust the seasonings of the dish after the cooking is completed. The balance of flavors tends to shift in this method of cooking.

THE CASSEROLE AND THE DUTCH OVEN

The terms casserole and Dutch oven are often used interchangeably to describe a large, heavy, covered pot, which can be used in the oven as well as on top of the stove. Terminology becomes even more confused by the French usage of *casserole,* which literally means "saucepan."

In this book the term casserole is used to mean a deep dish of any heatproof material without a long handle, suitable for baking and roasting, and if flameproof, for top-of-the-stove cooking. It should have a fitted lid and, if made of clay or another porous material, should be sealed. By Dutch oven, this book refers to a large, heavy casserole or pot, made of metal, with a fitted lid, which may be used for browning, as well as cooking either on top of the stove or in the oven.

Historically the casserole has its origins in the ancient earthenware pot which, when treated with plant gum, became waterproof. Many of our modern casseroles are both heatproof and flameproof. However, a casserole which is merely heatproof may usually be adapted for stovetop cooking

8

with an asbestos pad. When purchasing a new casserole for oven-to-table use, do make certain that the materials used are safe. Slow poisoning from improperly fired ceramic casseroles can occur.

The origins of the Dutch oven have been obscured by history, but there is evidence of the widespread use during the American Colonial period of large iron stewing pots which were hung on hooks over the kitchen fire or set on coals in the hearth. In today's kitchen, the Dutch oven is made of cast iron, aluminum, stainless steel or other metal, or porcelain enamelware and is useful as a roaster, soup pot, casserole or deep fryer. If your Dutch oven is made of cast iron, follow the care instructions at the end of this chapter.

THE SLOW COOKER

The slow cooker phenomenon comes as no surprise to the chef who has salvaged a poor cut of meat by simmering it slowly and basting it often. The slow cooker provides its own "moist environment," eliminating the need for basting; the cover should not be lifted until the prescribed cooking period has ended.

A high-glaze finish and the enclosure of the electric heating elements on the sides of most slow cookers prevent sticking or burning. Some models have browning units, but if yours does not, meats should be browned first in a separate pan.

For safe cooking, the temperature of the slow cooker must reach 165° within three to four hours of the beginning of the cooking time. This will minimize any growth of bacteria in the foods. Slow cookers that take too long to heat encourage bacteria growth which can cause the food to spoil.

Although the slow cooker operates at low wattage, the long cooking times make the energy consumption about the same as when the dish is cooked on an electric range. However, there is little steam generated, so valuable vitamins and minerals are retained with the slow cooker.

Some slow cookers have electric elements which may be detached for cleaning. Warm soapy water may generally be used to clean the inside of the pot. Because constructions and finishes vary, follow the manufacturer's instructions for cleaning.

While hardly a temperamental kitchen companion, certain proprieties about the slow cooker should be observed. Lifting the lid during cooking lowers the interior temperature, resulting in undercooked food or an increase in the cooking time. The cooker should be at least half full or the proper cooking temperature will not be reached. A few vegetables may be added at the end of the cooking period and cooked on high for last-minute finish. Follow the recipes precisely on this score. If excess liquid remains at end of cooking, reduce over high heat. Adjust seasonings of each dish before serving.

THE WET CLAY COOKER

The wet clay cooker, now undergoing a revival stimulated by the promotion efforts of several ambitious West German manufacturers, is an old method of cooking. The notion of clay as a protective, moisture-sealing cooking material belongs to the North American Indians, who wrapped wet

A PRIMER OF POTS

clay around fish, threw it into the fire until it hardened, and cracked it open when the contents were presumed done. The Romans carried the use of clay for cooking vessels to its ultimate, using clay extensively though other materials were available to them.

In its modern form, the wet clay cooker is usually oval-shaped with ridges on the inside of the bottom to hold the contents slightly above the juices, thus preventing sticking. It has a fitted top with a small space for escaping steam. The wet clay cooker has an unglazed finish throughout and must be soaked in water before each use. It may be seasoned periodically by rubbing it with garlic and adding whatever herbs are desired to the soaking water. Soaking the clay before cooking allows water to fill the "pores"; the water forms a moist haze during cooking, eliminating the need for basting or excess liquids or fats.

The wet clay cooker has the advantage of cooking its contents in natural juices, retaining the original vitamins and nutrients, and is attractive enough for oven-to-table presentation. Avoid sudden temperature changes, remembering to start with a cold oven and to add warm liquids only after the contents have been warmed. Set the finished dish on a towel rather than a cold stone or metal surface.

As recommended by the manufacturer, use the wet clay cooker only in the oven. Even an

asbestos pad is ineffective in converting some wet clay cookers to stovetop use, but a dish may be browned in the oven by removing lid for the last 10 minutes of cooking. Wash with warm soapy water after use. Store the cooker with lid turned upside down. If desired, cooking fat may be omitted in the recipes using this pot.

THE SKILLET

The skillet is a catchall term in the modern kitchen, covering every utensil from the *saucier,* or saucepan, to the omelet pan. In the mid-19th century, a skillet was known as a "spider" and came equipped with tapered legs and a long handle; when the kitchen range became a culinary fact of life, the skillet's legs were cut off to allow it to rest directly on the heat source.

Skillets come in many materials: cast iron, aluminum, stainless steel, copper, rolled or carbon steel, porcelain enamelware, non-stick finishes and heat-resistant glass. If using a skillet of cast iron or rolled or carbon steel, follow the directions for its care at the end of this chapter.

THE WOK

The wok was devised by the Chinese to permit fast cooking at high heat while using very little fuel. Its rounded bottom distributes heat evenly and efficiently and permits cooking of large or small quantities of food in the same pan. The round shape also makes it easier to stir-fry bulky items without spilling. Woks come with a single wooden handle or double metal handles, with or without a lid or ring base. The wooden-handled models are easier to cook with, but the smaller metal handles are less hazardous, need less storage space and may also be used in the oven or over charcoal. Flat-bottom woks are recommended for use on electric stoves. Most woks are made of rolled steel and should be seasoned and cared for according to the directions at the end of this chapter.

THE OMELET PAN

The omelet pan is a type of skillet with a long handle and sloping sides to facilitate sliding the omelet from the pan. Many chefs consider them a necessity, but a skillet may also be effectively used for preparing omelets. Traditionally the French omelet pan is made of carbon steel, but today's market offers models in cast iron, aluminum, stainless steel, porcelain enamelware and the new nonstick surfaces. Carbon steel or cast-iron pans should be seasoned and cared for according to the directions at the end of this chapter.

THE STOCKPOT OR SOUP POT

The traditional stockpot or soup pot is taller than its diameter, thus reducing evaporation by exposing a small surface to the air. The height of the pot also allows the ingredients to boil up through the simmering stock. However, a Dutch oven or large saucepan may always be substituted for a stockpot or soup pot. The stockpot is more versatile than it appears at first glance. With a rack it can be converted to a steamer.

THE SOUFFLÉ

The soufflé dish, startling in its simplicity, is the perfect oven-to-table item. It should have straight sides, ridged on the outside and a flat bottom. Its capacity may vary from one pint (individual ramekins are much smaller) to several quarts. Determine the capacity of yours by measuring the amount of liquid it holds up to the indentation line.

In several of the following recipes, a deep casserole may be substituted for the soufflé. However, even the plainest soufflé dish is so attractive that a dozen other table-top uses come to mind. The usual precautions against sudden temperature changes prevail with the soufflé (see Wet Clay Cooker).

CARE OF ROLLED OR CARBON STEEL AND CAST-IRON COOKWARE

Carbon or rolled steel and cast-iron cookware require seasoning and special care. To season a new pot, first wash it thoroughly with detergent and hot water. Rinse well and dry the pot over heat. Then rub the inside with cooking oil, such as peanut or corn oil, and place it over high heat for one minute. Rinse in hot water and dry over heat. Rub with oil again and wipe out excess oil with paper toweling. Repeat oil application. Place over heat and wipe out with paper toweling. Repeat until paper remains clean, then rinse in hot water and dry over heat. Rub lightly with oil before storing. After each use, wash immediately with hot water and a stiff brush and dry over heat. Never use a metal scouring pad. Reseason with oil as needed.

SOUPS

BLACK BEAN SOUP

Serves 6
2 onions, chopped
2 cloves garlic, minced
3 tablespoons butter
1 pound black beans, washed,
   soaked overnight and drained
1 ham bone, cracked
1 celery rib with some leaves, chopped
1 bay leaf
1/2 cup Madeira or sherry
salt and freshly ground pepper to taste
garnish:
   2 hard-cooked eggs, finely chopped
   chopped parsley
   thin lemon slices

Top-of-the-Stove Method
In a soup pot sauté the onions and garlic in butter until transparent. Add the beans, ham bone, celery, bay leaf and 3 quarts water. Bring to a boil, skim surface scum, lower heat and simmer, covered, for 4 hours. Remove ham bone and bay leaf. Purée soup and return to pot. Add Madeira, salt and pepper and heat through. Serve in soup bowls garnished with eggs, parsley and lemon slices.

Slow Cooker Method
Sauté onions and garlic in butter until transparent in a skillet or a slow cooker with a browning unit. Combine with beans, ham bone, celery, bay leaf and 2 quarts water in a slow cooker. Cover and cook on high 2 hours. Turn heat to low and cook, covered, 8 to 10 hours. Proceed as directed for top-of-the-stove method.

SOUPS

TUSCAN BEAN SOUP

Serves 6 to 8
2 tablespoons olive oil
1 clove garlic, minced
1 onion, chopped
1 carrot, chopped
1 celery rib, chopped
2 leeks, chopped
1 sprig rosemary, finely chopped
1 fresh green chili pepper, seeded and minced
1 pound dried white beans, washed,
   soaked overnight and drained
1 ham bone, cracked
salt and freshly ground pepper to taste
garnish:
   1/2 cup grated Parmesan cheese
   1 onion, thinly sliced

Top-of-the-Stove Method
Heat oil in a large soup pot and sauté garlic, onion, carrot, celery, leeks, rosemary and chili pepper until just browned. Add beans, ham bone and 3 quarts water; simmer, covered, for 2 hours. Season with salt and pepper. Remove ham bone and rub half the beans through a fine sieve (or purée in a blender). Return purée to the soup and heat through. Serve in soup bowls, garnished with cheese and onion.

Slow Cooker Method
Sauté garlic, onion, carrot, celery, leeks, rosemary and chili pepper in oil until just browned in a skillet or a slow cooker with a browning unit. Combine with beans, ham bone and 2 quarts water in a slow cooker. Cover and cook on high 2 hours. Turn heat to low and cook, covered, 8 to 10 hours. Season with salt and pepper and proceed as directed for top-of-the-stove method.

MINESTRONE, MILANESE STYLE

Serves 6 to 8
1/4 pound salt pork, diced
1 clove garlic, minced
1 onion, thinly sliced
2 sprigs parsley, chopped
1/2 cup small dried white beans, washed,
    soaked overnight and drained
2 potatoes, peeled and cubed
2 carrots, diced
2 celery ribs, sliced
2 medium-sized zucchini, thinly sliced
2 ripe tomatoes, peeled and chopped
1 small head cabbage, shredded
1 cup fresh peas (1 pound, unshelled)
1/2 cup rice
salt and freshly ground pepper to taste
1 tablespoon chopped basil
garnish: grated Parmesan cheese
accompaniment. crusty Italian or French bread

Top-of-the-Stove Method
In a soup pot sauté salt pork, garlic, onion and parsley over medium heat. Add beans and 3 quarts of water. Put remaining vegetables into pot, except for cabbage and peas; bring to a boil. Lower heat, cover and simmer for 1-1/2 hours. Add cabbage, peas and rice and cook for 20 minutes, or until rice is tender. Add salt, pepper and basil, top with grated Parmesan and serve in individual bowls, accompanied with French bread

Slow Cooker Method
Sauté the salt pork, garlic, onion and parsley in a skillet or a slow cooker with a browning unit. Combine with all remaining ingredients, except cabbage, peas, rice and basil, and 2 quarts water in a slow cooker. Cover and cook on high 2 hours. Turn heat to low and cook, covered, 8 hours. Add cabbage, peas and rice and cook on high 30 minutes or until rice is tender. Serve as directed for top-of-the-stove method.

SOUPS

HAM AND LENTIL SOUP

Serves 6
2 cups lentils
1/2 pound ham, diced
1 onion, coarsely chopped
1 bay leaf
2 celery ribs, coarsely chopped
1 clove garlic, minced
salt and freshly ground pepper to taste

Top-of-the-Stove Method
Combine all the ingredients with 2 quarts water in a soup pot and bring to a boil. Reduce heat and simmer, covered, for 1-1/2 to 2 hours. Adjust seasonings and serve.

Slow Cooker Method
Combine all ingredients with 2 quarts water in a slow cooker. Cook on low, covered, 8 to 10 hours. Adjust seasonings and serve.

Variation The soup may be served puréed. Blend 2 cups at a time in the blender, return to the soup pot and heat through.

LAMB AND RED LENTIL SOUP

Serves 6
1 large onion, chopped
1 clove garlic, minced
3 tablespoons olive oil
4 cups chopped Swiss chard
2 cups red lentils
2 lamb shanks
1-1/2 teaspoons salt
1/2 teaspoon freshly ground pepper
1/4 cup fresh lemon juice

Top-of-the-Stove Method
In a soup pot sauté onion and garlic in olive oil until limp; add Swiss chard and stir until wilted; remove from pan and set aside. In the same pot, combine lentils, lamb shanks, salt, pepper and 2 quarts water and bring to a boil; reduce heat, cover and simmer 1 hour. Add Swiss chard mixture to pot and simmer for 15 minutes. Add lemon juice, adjust seasonings and serve. Lamb shanks may be served on the side or meat may be removed from bones, diced and returned to soup.

Slow Cooker Method
Sauté onion and garlic in oil until limp in a skillet or a slow cooker with a browning unit. Combine with remaining ingredients, except lemon juice, and 2 quarts water in a slow cooker. Cover and cook on low 8 to 10 hours. Add lemon juice and proceed as directed for top-of-the-stove method.

PESTO SOUP

Serves 6 to 8

1 pound small dried white beans, washed, soaked
  overnight and drained
1 potato, peeled and diced
2 carrots, diced
2 leeks, diced
2 tomatoes, peeled, seeded and diced
1/4 pound green beans, diced
2 zucchini, diced
2 sage leaves, minced, or
1/4 teaspoon powdered sage
1 teaspoon salt
1/2 teaspoon freshly ground pepper
2 ounces vermicelli

Pesto Sauce

3 cloves garlic, minced
6 basil leaves, minced
1/2 cup grated Parmesan cheese
1/4 cup olive oil

Top-of-the-Stove Method

Place beans in a soup pot with 3 quarts of water
and bring to a boil. Skim off any scum that appears
on the surface, lower heat, cover and simmer 1
hour. Add the potato, carrots, leeks, tomatoes,
green beans, zucchini, sage, salt and pepper and
continue simmering, covered, for another hour.
Add the vermicelli and cook for 15 minutes. Mix
the garlic, basil, Parmesan cheese and olive oil.
Remove the soup from the heat and stir in the
sauce. Serve immediately.

Slow Cooker Method

Combine all ingredients except vermicelli and sauce
in a slow cooker with 2 quarts water. Cover and
cook on high 2 hours. Turn heat to low and cook,
covered, 8 hours. Add vermicelli, turn on high and
cook, covered, 30 minutes. Combine sauce ingredients, stir into soup and serve.

SOUPS

MANHATTAN CLAM CHOWDER

Serves 6

2 slices bacon, diced
2 onions, chopped
2 celery ribs with some leaves, chopped
2 tablespoons chopped parsley
4 cups peeled and chopped ripe tomatoes
1 teaspoon dried thyme
1 bay leaf
1 pint clams, drained (reserve liquor) and
   coarsely chopped

3 potatoes, peeled and cut into 1/2-inch cubes
salt and freshly ground pepper to taste
accompaniment: pilot crackers

Fry the bacon in a large saucepan or soup pot just to release fat. Add onions and sauté until transparent; then add celery, parsley, tomatoes, thyme, bay leaf, reserved clam liquor and 6 cups water. Bring to a boil, reduce heat and simmer covered for 30 minutes. Add potatoes, cover and cook for 20 minutes, or until potatoes are tender. Add clams; simmer 10 minutes longer. Season with salt and pepper. Serve with pilot crackers.

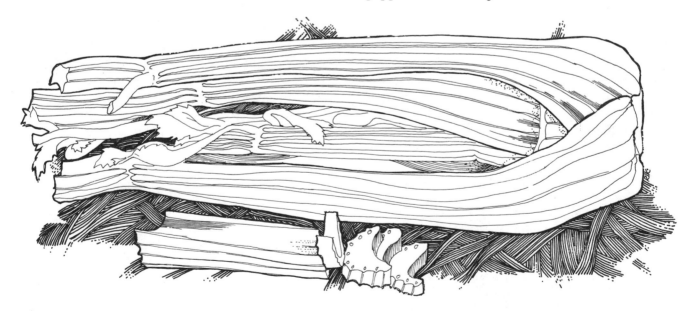

NEW ENGLAND CLAM CHOWDER

Serves 6
1 quart clams with liquor
1/4 pound salt pork, well rinsed and diced, or
2 slices bacon, diced
1 onion, chopped
3 potatoes, peeled and cut into 1/2-inch cubes
3 tablespoons butter
1 pint half-and-half, or
1 cup each milk and heavy cream
salt and white pepper to taste
accompaniment: pilot crackers

Combine clams and their liquor and 1 quart water. Bring just to a boil in a large saucepan or soup pot. Drain clams and reserve liquid; chop clams coarsely and set aside. Fry the salt pork or bacon just to release fat; add onion and cook until onion is transparent. Add the reserved liquid and potatoes and cook covered until potatoes are tender, about 20 minutes. Stir in butter, half-and-half, reserved clams, salt and pepper. Heat through; do not boil. Serve with pilot crackers.

SOUPS

SEAFOOD GUMBO

Serves 6
1 pound shrimp, shelled and deveined,
   shells reserved
1 pound fish heads and scraps
1 bay leaf
2 whole allspice
1 onion, chopped
2 cloves garlic, minced
3 tablespoons butter
2 cups peeled and chopped tomatoes
1 pound okra, sliced
1 pound firm white fish fillets, cut into chunks
1 pint oysters, drained (reserve liquor)
1 teaspoon salt
1/2 teaspoon freshly ground pepper
pinch of cayenne pepper
accompaniment: 3 cups freshly cooked rice

In a soup pot combine shrimp shells, fish head and scraps, bay leaf, allspice and 2 quarts water. Bring to a boil and simmer 30 minutes. Strain, discard shells and fish scraps and set broth aside. Sauté onion and garlic in soup pot in butter for 5 minutes. Add reserved broth, tomatoes and okra. Bring to a boil and simmer 30 minutes. Add shrimp, fish, oysters and their liquor, salt, pepper and cayenne. Cook for 15 minutes and serve in individual soup plates with rice.

SALT COD SOUP

Serves 6
1 pound salt cod, soaked in water to cover for
   2 hours and drained
3 tablespoons olive oil
2 onions, thinly sliced
2 cloves garlic, minced
1 bay leaf
2 sprigs thyme, or
1 teaspoon dried thyme
1 celery rib, chopped
1/4 cup chopped parsley
2 cups peeled and chopped ripe tomatoes
1 cup dry white wine
4 potatoes, peeled and quartered
freshly ground pepper to taste
garnish: chopped parsley and grated
   Parmesan cheese
accompaniment: crusty French or Italian bread

Cut cod into 2-1/2-inch pieces; set aside. Heat oil in soup pot or large saucepan and sauté onions and garlic until golden. Add bay leaf, thyme, celery, parsley and tomatoes and simmer for 10 minutes. Add wine, potatoes, reserved cod and 6 cups water; simmer for about 30 minutes. Season with pepper. Serve garnished with parsley and cheese and accompany with French or Italian bread.

CHICKEN AND CORN CHOWDER

Serves 6
2 slices bacon, diced
1 onion, chopped
1 3-pound fryer chicken, cut up
1 bay leaf
1 teaspoon salt
1/2 teaspoon white pepper
4 cups freshly grated corn kernels
1 cup chopped celery
1 cup evaporated milk
garnish:
    2 hard-cooked eggs, chopped
    chopped parsley

In soup pot or large saucepan fry bacon just to release fat; remove bacon bits with a slotted spoon and sauté onions in drippings until golden. Place chicken in the pot and add 3 quarts water. Bring to a rapid boil and skim any surface scum. Add bay leaf, salt and pepper. Lower heat and simmer covered for 1 hour. Remove chicken pieces; add corn kernels and celery and return bacon to the pot. Continue simmering covered for 30 minutes. Meanwhile, bone chicken and discard bones and fat (or save for chicken stock). Dice meat and return to the pot with the evaporated milk. Heat through and serve in warmed soup bowls, garnished with chopped eggs and parsley.

CHICKEN-NOODLE SOUP

Serves 4 to 6
1 3-pound whole fryer chicken, with giblets
1 celery rib, with leaves
2 carrots
1 onion, stuck with 2 cloves
1 bay leaf
8 ounces egg noodles
2 sprigs parsley, chopped
salt and freshly ground pepper to taste

In a soup pot combine chicken, celery, carrots, onion and bay leaf with 3 quarts water. Bring to a boil, skim off any surface scum, lower heat, cover and simmer 1-1/2 hours. Remove chicken, strain broth and return broth to pot. Add noodles and continue cooking, uncovered, over medium heat for 10 minutes. Add parsley, salt and pepper. Chicken may be cut up and served separately, or boned, diced and returned to pot.

Variations
• For chicken-rice soup, substitute 1 cup rice for noodles and cook for 20 minutes.
• For chicken-vegetable soup, chop the vegetables and add 1 tomato, peeled, seeded and diced; do not strain broth.

SOUPS

HAITIAN CHICKEN-IN-THE-POT

Serves 4 to 6
1 3-1/2- to 4-pound whole fryer chicken
1 pound ham hocks
1/2 cup fresh orange juice
1 onion, stuck with 2 cloves
2 carrots, halved
1 small head cabbage, cut in wedges
1/2 pound summer squash
1 celery rib, halved
2 tablespoons vinegar

Top-of-the-Stove Method
In a soup pot combine the chicken, ham hocks, orange juice and onion with water to cover (about 3 quarts). Bring to a rapid boil and skim any surface scum. Lower heat, cover and simmer for 1 hour. Add carrots, cabbage, squash, celery and vinegar and simmer for 30 minutes. Remove the meats and vegetables and place on a warm platter. Strain broth and serve separately.

Pressure Cooker Method
In a pressure cooker combine the chicken, ham hocks, orange juice and onion with water to cover, no more than two-thirds capacity. Cover and bring to full pressure. When steam appears, reduce heat and cook on low 15 minutes. Reduce pressure completely, uncover and add carrots, cabbage, squash, celery and vinegar. Cover and simmer for 30 minutes, not under pressure. Let stand covered 10 to 15 minutes to blend flavors. Remove the meats and vegetables and place on a warm platter. Strain broth and serve separately.

POT-AU-FEU

Serves 8 to 10
1 beef knuckle bone
1 3-pound beef brisket or rump
1 bay leaf
2 sprigs parsley
2 sprigs thyme, or
1 teaspoon dried thyme
1 whole plump chicken, about 4 pounds
1 pound chicken giblets
6 carrots, halved
3 leeks, white part only
2 onions, each stuck with 2 cloves
3 turnips, quartered
3 celery ribs with some leaves, halved
salt and freshly ground pepper to taste
accompaniments:
    pickles and horseradish
    French bread and sweet butter

Top-of-the-Stove Method
In a soup pot, bring knuckle bone and beef brisket to a boil in 4 quarts of water. Skim off any surface scum and add bay leaf, parsley and thyme. Lower heat and simmer covered for 1-1/2 hours. Add chicken, giblets, carrots, leeks, onions, turnips and celery. Bring to a boil, cover, lower heat and simmer for 45 minutes or until chicken is tender. Season with salt and pepper. Put meats and chicken on a platter with the giblets; surround with vegetables and keep warm. Strain the broth, skimming off fat, and serve separately in cups. Slice meat and serve accompanied with pickles and horseradish. Serve with French bread and butter.

Slow Cooker Method
Combine all ingredients with only 3 quarts water and cook on low, covered, for 8 to 10 hours. Serve as directed for top-of-the-stove method.

SOUPS

MULLIGATAWNY

Serves 6
1-1/2 pounds mutton or lamb stewing meat,
    cut into 1/2-inch dice
4 tablespoons butter
1 onion, minced
1 tablespoon curry powder
2 tablespoons flour
1/3 cup lentils
2 tart apples, peeled and diced
1 bell pepper, diced
2 carrots, diced
1 teaspoon sugar
1/2 teaspoon ground mace
1/4 teaspoon ground cloves
salt and freshly ground pepper to taste
1 cup coconut milk, following
accompaniment: freshly cooked rice

Top-of-the-Stove Method

Brown the meat in the butter in a soup pot; add onion, curry powder and flour and cook and stir for 2 minutes. Add 3 quarts of water and remaining ingredients except for coconut milk. Bring to a boil, lower heat and simmer for 1-1/2 hours. Add coconut milk and heat through; do not boil. Serve in individual soup bowls with rice to be added, as much as desired, to each serving.

Slow Cooker Method

Brown the meat in butter in a skillet or a slow cooker with a browning unit. Add onion, curry powder and flour and cook and stir for 2 minutes. Combine with remaining ingredients, except coconut milk, and 2 quarts water in a slow cooker. Cover and cook on low 8 to 10 hours. Add coconut milk, heat through and serve with rice.

Coconut Milk

For each cup of coconut milk needed, combine 1 cup unsweetened grated coconut and 1 cup milk in a pan and bring to a boil. Remove from heat, cool and press through a sieve. Coconut milk is also available in cans.

VEGETABLE AND BEEF BARLEY SOUP

Serves 6
2 pounds lean beef short ribs
2 cups peeled and chopped tomatoes
1 teaspoon salt
1 bay leaf
1 cup green beans, cut into 1-inch lengths
1 cup freshly grated corn kernels
1 onion, chopped
1/2 cup pearl barley
1/2 teaspoon dried oregano
1/2 teaspoon dried basil
1 clove garlic, crushed

Place short ribs, tomatoes, salt and bay leaf in a large soup pot; add 2 quarts water. Cover and bring to a rapid boil; skim any surface scum. Reduce heat and simmer, covered, for 2 hours. Add remaining ingredients and simmer 1 hour, or until meat is tender. Remove short ribs from soup, cut meat from bones, dice meat and add to soup; heat through. Skim surface fat again before serving.

SOUPS

HUNGARIAN MEATBALL SOUP

Serves 4
1 pound lean ground beef
1 cup bread crumbs
1 egg, beaten
salt and freshly ground pepper to taste
1 onion, thinly sliced
2 tablespoons butter
1 teaspoon paprika
2 cups peeled and diced potatoes
garnish:
    sour cream or plain yogurt
    chopped parsley

Combine the beef, bread crumbs, egg, salt and pepper. Shape into 1-inch balls. In a saucepan sauté the onion in butter until soft, then add the paprika and 4 cups water. Bring to a rapid boil, lower heat and add meatballs and potatoes. Cover and simmer 30 minutes. Ladle into soup bowls, top each with a spoonful of sour cream or yogurt and sprinkle parsley on top.

OXTAIL AND VEGETABLE SOUP

Serves 6
3 pounds oxtails, disjointed and
    parboiled 5 minutes
1 bay leaf
1 onion, chopped
2 leeks, chopped
2 celery ribs with leaves, chopped
3 carrots, diced
3 turnips, diced
3 beets, diced
2 ripe tomatoes, peeled and chopped
2 cups chopped cabbage, spinach or Swiss chard
2 sprigs parsley, chopped
1 teaspoon salt
1/2 teaspoon freshly ground pepper
accompaniment: French bread

Place oxtails in a large soup pot with 3 quarts water. Bring to boil and skim off any surface scum. Add remaining ingredients, lower heat, cover and simmer for 1-1/2 hours. Adjust seasonings and remove bay leaf. Serve with French bread.

SOPA DE ALBONDIGAS
(Mexican Meatball Soup)

Serves 4 to 6
1/2 pound each lean ground beef and pork
1/4 cup rice
1/2 teaspoon chili powder
1 teaspoon salt
1/2 teaspoon freshly ground pepper
1/4 teaspoon ground cumin
1 egg
1 onion, chopped
1 clove garlic, minced
3 tablespoons olive oil
2 quarts beef stock
1 cup peeled and chopped ripe tomatoes
garnish: chopped parsley or coriander
accompaniment: tortillas or French bread

Combine the beef, pork, rice, seasonings and egg. Shape into small balls the size of a walnut. Set aside. Sauté the onion and garlic in olive oil until golden. Add the stock and tomatoes. Bring to a rapid boil, drop in meatballs and cook, covered, over medium heat for 25 minutes. Ladle into warmed soup bowls and garnish with parsley or coriander. Serve with tortillas or French bread.

SCOTCH BROTH

Serves 6 to 8
1 leftover lamb bone, with some meat remaining, or
2 pounds lamb shoulder or neck
1 onion, diced
2 carrots, diced
1 celery rib with some leaves, diced
1/4 cup chopped parsley
1 bay leaf
1/4 teaspoon cayenne pepper
1 teaspoon dried thyme
1/2 cup pearl barley
salt and freshly ground pepper to taste

Put the lamb bone, shoulder or neck in a soup pot with 3 quarts of water. Bring to a rapid boil and skim any surface scum. Add remaining ingredients, bring back to a boil and simmer, covered, for 2 hours. Remove lamb bone, scrape and dice meat, and return meat to pot. Serve very hot in deep soup bowls.

EGGS & CHEESE

BAKED EGGS WITH PARMESAN CHEESE

Serves 3 or 4
2 tablespoons butter
1/2 cup grated Parmesan cheese
6 eggs
1 cup plain yogurt
salt and pepper to taste
6 slices rye bread toast
optional accompaniment: sliced tomatoes and
   bell pepper strips in vinaigrette

Butter a shallow baking dish with 1 teaspoon of
the butter and sprinkle half the cheese over the
bottom. Carefully break the eggs into the dish,
spacing them evenly over the cheese surface, and
spoon the yogurt over the eggs. Salt and pepper
lightly. Sprinkle remaining cheese on top of eggs.
Dot with remaining butter and bake in a preheated
350° oven for 15 minutes. Serve over toast with
tomatoes and bell pepper strips, if desired.

ZUCCHINI, POTATO AND CHEESE CASSEROLE

Serves 4
1 pound zucchini, thinly sliced
3 potatoes, peeled and thinly sliced
2 cups grated Monterey Jack cheese
1 cup bread crumbs
1/2 cup chopped parsley
2 cloves garlic, minced
3 tablespoons olive oil
3 tablespoons butter
salt and freshly ground pepper to taste

Butter an earthenware 1-1/2-quart casserole or baking dish and layer with one-third of the zucchini
and potato slices. Sprinkle with one-third of the
cheese, bread crumbs, parsley, garlic, salt, pepper
and drizzle with 1 tablespoon of the oil. Repeat
each layer twice, drizzling each with oil. Dot top
with butter and pour 1/4 cup water over all. Cover
and bake in a preheated 350° oven for 1 hour.

EGGS & CHEESE

CHEESE AND CORN PIE

Serves 8
2 onions, chopped
1/4 cup corn oil
2 tomatoes, peeled and diced
1 cup unbleached white flour
3/4 cup yellow cornmeal
1 tablespoon baking powder
1 teaspoon salt
2 tablespoons sugar
1 egg
1 cup milk
4 tablespoons butter, melted
2 cups freshly grated corn kernels, or
1 1-pound can creamed-style corn
3 eggs, separated and at room temperature
1/2 pound Monterey Jack cheese, grated

Sauté onions in oil until transparent; add tomatoes and cook for 5 minutes. Set aside. Sift together flour, cornmeal, baking powder, salt and sugar. Add whole egg, milk and butter to flour mixture and blend well. Add corn, egg yolks, cheese and onion-tomato mixture to flour mixture. Beat egg whites until stiff but not dry and fold into flour mixture. Bake in a buttered 2-quart casserole in a preheated 300° oven for 1 hour, or until firm.

ASPARAGUS-HAM-AND-CHEESE TORTE

Serves 6
2 pounds asparagus, thinly sliced on diagonal
   and parboiled 2 minutes
2 cups shredded cooked ham
1 cup grated Cheddar cheese
salt and freshly ground pepper to taste
2 cups milk
3 eggs, beaten
dash of freshly grated nutmeg

Generously butter a 2-quart casserole or baking dish and make layers of half the asparagus, ham and cheese. Season with salt and pepper. Repeat layers. Combine milk and eggs and pour over all. Sprinkle with nutmeg and place in a preheated 350° oven for 35 minutes, or until set.

Variations
In place of asparagus, use:
• 2 pounds zucchini, sliced and parboiled 2 minutes
• 2 bunches spinach, blanched and chopped
• 2 pounds broccoli, trimmed, coarsely chopped and parboiled 2 minutes
In place of ham, use:
• cooked shredded chicken or turkey
• cooked shrimp or crab meat

RICE, GREEN CHILIES AND CHEESE CASSEROLE

Serves 4
3 cups cooked rice
1 7-1/2-ounce can whole green chilies,
    coarsely chopped
3 cups grated Monterey Jack cheese
3 medium-sized zucchini, thinly sliced and
    parboiled for 3 minutes
1 large tomato, thinly sliced
salt and freshly ground pepper to taste
2 cups (1 pint) sour cream
1 teaspoon dried oregano
1 clove garlic, minced
1/4 cup chopped bell pepper
1/4 cup chopped green onion
garnish: 2 tablespoons chopped parsley

In a buttered 3-quart casserole, place cooked rice and cover with chilies. Sprinkle half of the grated cheese over rice and arrange zucchini slices on top. Add tomato slices and lightly salt and pepper. Combine sour cream, oregano, garlic, bell pepper and onion. Spoon evenly over tomatoes and sprinkle with remaining cheese. Bake in a preheated 350° oven for 45 minutes, or until heated through. Sprinkle with parsley and serve immediately.

CHICKEN LIVERS AND EGGS ON TOAST

Serves 4
3 tablespoons butter
1/2 pound chicken livers, halved
2 tablespoons chopped onion
1/3 cup dry white wine
1 teaspoon tomato paste
4 eggs
freshly made toast, preferably French bread
salt and freshly ground pepper to taste
freshly grated nutmeg

In a skillet over medium heat, melt butter and sauté the chicken livers with onion until livers lose their redness, about 5 minutes. Stir in wine and tomato paste. Break eggs into pan, one at a time, being careful not to break yolks. Cover and cook over low heat for 2 minutes or until whites are just firm and yolks are soft. Serve hot on toast; sprinkle with salt and pepper and nutmeg.

EGGS & CHEESE

MEAT-AND-TOMATO CAKE

Serves 6
1 pound lean ground beef
1 large onion, chopped
1 clove garlic, minced
2 tablespoons olive oil
1/2 teaspoon each salt and freshly
    ground pepper
2 tomatoes, peeled and chopped
1/3 cup finely chopped parsley
1 teaspoon ground cumin
2 tablespoons chopped mint, or
2 teaspoons dried mint
4 eggs, beaten

In a skillet brown beef, onion and garlic in oil; add salt, pepper, tomatoes, parsley, cumin and mint. Cook over low heat, stirring constantly. Blend eggs into meat mixture and cook over low heat until eggs are set. Cut into wedges to serve.

RICE FRITTATA

Serves 6
3 cups cooked rice
3 cups chopped cooked vegetables (zucchini,
    spinach and/or asparagus may be used)
2 tablespoons chopped green onions
1 teaspoon dried oregano
2 teaspoons chopped basil, or
3/4 teaspoon dried basil
1/2 cup grated Parmesan cheese
1 cup grated Monterey Jack cheese
4 eggs, beaten
1/4 cup olive oil
salt and freshly ground pepper to taste

Combine all ingredients and pour into a buttered 2-quart casserole. Bake in preheated 350° oven for 25 minutes, or until eggs are set. Cut into squares and serve hot or cold.

Variations Add 1/2 cup chopped cooked ham, chicken or veal before baking.

SCRAMBLED EGGS WITH OYSTERS

Serves 4 to 5
8 eggs
1/4 teaspoon salt
dash of freshly ground pepper
5 tablespoons butter
1 7-ounce can oysters, rinsed and well drained
accompaniment: toasted bread

Beat together the eggs and salt and pepper. Melt butter in a skillet, pour in eggs and cook until they begin to set; stir gently with a fork. Add oysters and continue cooking until eggs are soft and creamy. Serve hot, over toast if desired.

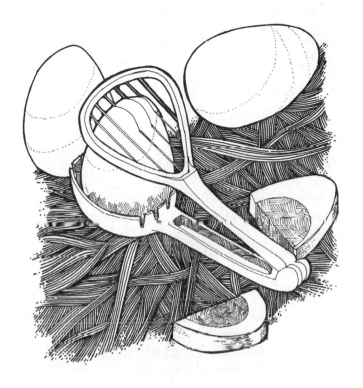

EGGS & CHEESE

CHEESE SOUFFLÉ

Serves 4 to 6
1/4 pound butter
1/2 cup unbleached white flour
2 cups milk
2 cups grated Cheddar cheese
1/2 teaspoon paprika
1 teaspoon dry mustard
8 eggs, separated and at room temperature

Melt butter in a double boiler; blend in flour until the mixture is smooth. Stir in milk slowly and cook until the mixture thickens. Blend in grated cheese and seasonings. Stir until the cheese melts, and remove from heat. Beat the egg yolks well and stir into the cheese mixture. Beat the egg whites until stiff but not dry and fold carefully into the mixture. Turn into a buttered 2-quart soufflé dish or deep casserole. Place in a pan of hot water and bake in a preheated 350° oven 50 to 60 minutes, or until golden brown. Serve at once.

VEGETABLE SOUFFLÉ

Serves 4 to 6
1 small onion, chopped
6 tablespoons butter
5 tablespoons quick-cooking tapioca
1-1/2 cups milk
4 eggs, separated and at room temperature
1/2 teaspoon salt
pinch of freshly ground pepper
2 cups chopped cooked vegetable, such as spinach,
    broccoli, cauliflower, green beans, peas,
    carrots, corn, zucchini, asparagus,
    artichoke hearts or any combination
1 cup grated sharp Cheddar cheese

In a saucepan sauté onion in butter for 5 minutes. Add tapioca, milk, egg yolks and salt and pepper. Cook over medium heat and bring to a boil, stirring constantly until thickened. Remove from heat, add vegetable and cheese and stir until cheese is melted. Beat egg whites until stiff but not dry. Fold egg whites gently into vegetable mixture and pour into a buttered 2-quart soufflé dish or casserole. Set in a pan of hot water and bake at 350° for 1 hour. Serve immediately.

HAM, CHEESE AND ASPARAGUS SOUFFLÉ

Serves 4
2 cups diced cooked ham
2 tablespoons chopped parsley
1 cup cooked coarsely cut asparagus
3 cups cooked elbow macaroni
1 cup grated Gruyère cheese
4 eggs, separated and at room temperature
1 cup heavy cream
1/2 teaspoon freshly grated nutmeg
1/2 teaspoon salt
1/4 teaspoon freshly ground pepper

Fit a lightly buttered, 1-1/2-quart soufflé dish with a 6-inch-wide band of foil or waxed paper, doubled to form a standing collar extending 2 inches above the rim. Butter the collar. Combine the ham, parsley, asparagus, macaroni and cheese. Beat the egg yolks and combine with the cream, nutmeg, salt and pepper. Blend yolk mixture with the ham mixture. In a separate bowl, beat the egg whites until stiff but not dry and fold into the ham mixture. Transfer into the prepared soufflé dish, set in a pan of hot water and bake in a preheated 375° oven for 35 to 40 minutes, or until puffed and brown. Remove the collar and serve the soufflé immediately.

Variations Substitute 2 cups diced cooked chicken, turkey, pork, veal or lamb for the ham.

RICOTTA CHEESE OMELET

Serves 4
1/4 cup olive oil
1/4 cup chopped onion
1 tablespoon chopped basil, or
1 teaspoon dried basil
1-1/2 cups peeled and chopped ripe tomatoes
1/2 pound (1 cup) ricotta cheese (cream-style cottage cheese may be substituted)
5 tablespoons grated Parmesan cheese
salt and freshly ground pepper to taste
2 tablespoons chopped parsley
6 eggs
3 tablespoons butter

Heat oil in an omelet pan or skillet. Add onion, basil and tomatoes and cook briskly for 20 minutes; remove to a side dish. Beat ricotta with 2 tablespoons of the Parmesan, the salt and parsley until smooth; set aside. Beat eggs with remaining Parmesan and season with salt and pepper; set aside. Heat the butter in omelet pan. Pour in egg mixture and cook over low heat until puffy. Pour ricotta mixture down middle and fold over both sides. Remove to a warm platter. Cover with tomato sauce and serve immediately.

EGGS & CHEESE

CHEESE AND RICE OMELET

Serves 4
6 eggs, separated
1/4 cup milk
1 cup cooked rice
salt and freshly ground pepper to taste
2 tablespoons each butter and corn oil
2 cups grated Monterey Jack cheese
3 tablespoons or more diced fresh green chilies
accompaniment: sliced tomatoes

Combine egg yolks and milk and beat well. Add rice and salt and pepper. Beat egg whites until stiff but not dry and fold into yolk mixture. Heat butter and oil in an omelet pan, pour in egg-rice mixture and cook over low heat until puffy. Sprinkle with grated cheese and chilies and place under broiler briefly until cheese melts. Cut into wedges and serve immediately.

BASQUE OMELET

Serves 4
1 2-ounce can anchovy fillets,
    drained and cut in small pieces
8 eggs, lightly beaten
3 tablespoons each butter and olive oil
1 green bell pepper, thinly sliced
1 sweet red pepper, thinly sliced
1 onion, thinly sliced
2 firm ripe tomatoes, peeled, seeded and diced
salt and freshly ground pepper to taste

Mix the anchovy pieces with the eggs; set aside. In a skillet heat the butter and oil over medium heat and sauté the peppers and onions for 5 minutes, or until vegetables are just wilted. Add the tomatoes and cook 5 minutes. Pour the egg-anchovy mixture over the vegetables and scramble until almost set and puffy. Stop scrambling and cook for 1-1/2 to 2 minutes, or until bottom is lightly golden. Turn out onto a warm platter, season with salt and pepper and serve immediately.

KOREAN MEAT-VEGETABLE PANCAKES

Serves 4
Pancakes
2 cups matchstick-cut zucchini or asparagus
1/2 cup chopped green onions
1/2 teaspoon salt
1/4 teaspoon pepper
1/4 cup unbleached white flour
6 eggs, beaten
1/2 pound lean ground pork, beef,
   chicken or shrimp
1/2 teaspoon Oriental sesame oil* (optional)
2 tablespoons peanut oil

Dipping Sauce
1/4 cup soy sauce
1 tablespoon rice vinegar or white vinegar
1 tablespoon sugar
1/4 teaspoon Oriental sesame oil (optional)
accompaniment: freshly cooked rice

Combine all of the ingredients for pancakes except
the peanut oil. Heat peanut oil in omelet pan or
skillet and drop 1 heaping tablespoonful of batter
into the oil for each pancake. Scrape the runny
edges to make a 3-inch pancake. Flip and fry on
the other side until golden, adding oil as needed.
Keep warm until all pancakes are made. Combine
ingredients for Dipping Sauce and serve with pancakes and rice.

*Available in Oriental markets.

GROUND BEEF, SPINACH AND EGGS

Serves 4
2 tablespoons each butter and olive oil
1/2 cup chopped onion
1 clove garlic, minced
1/2 pound lean ground beef
1 bunch spinach, blanched, chopped and
   well drained
6 eggs, lightly beaten
salt and freshly ground pepper to taste

Heat a skillet over medium heat, add butter and oil
and sauté the onion and garlic for 1 minute. Add
the beef, stirring constantly until the redness disap-
pears. Combine the spinach and eggs and pour over
the meat and onion mixture. Cook until the bottom begins to set, turning the uncooked eggs into
the center with a spatula. Continue cooking until
the eggs are almost set; do not overcook. Season
with salt and pepper.

SEAFOOD

CRAB CIOPPINO

Serves 4 to 6
2 live Dungeness crabs
3 cloves garlic, minced
2 onions, sliced
1/4 cup olive oil
1/2 pound Swiss chard, finely chopped
3 cups peeled and diced ripe tomatoes
2 cups tomato juice
1 cup dry white wine
1 tablespoon minced basil, or
1 teaspoon dried basil
1-1/2 teaspoons minced oregano, or
1/2 teaspoon dried oregano
1 small sprig rosemary, or
1/2 teaspoon dried rosemary
salt and freshly ground pepper to taste
accompaniment: sourdough French bread

Drop live crabs into boiling water and parboil for 2 minutes. Remove and plunge into cold water to end cooking process quickly. Cool for 5 minutes, then separate body and claws from shell; discard any soft spongy parts and the brown-yellow liquid inside shell. Split body in half and crack claws; set aside. Sauté garlic and onions in olive oil until onions are limp. Add the remaining ingredients and bring to a rapid boil. Lower heat and simmer for 15 minutes. Add the crab, cover and cook for 10 to 15 minutes; do not overcook. Serve immediately in large soup bowls, accompanied with sourdough French bread.

Seafood Cioppino Variation Substitute any combination of firm white fish, salmon, mussels, clams, shrimp, lobster or squid for the crab.

SEAFOOD

FISH STEW, GENOA STYLE

Serves 6
1/4 cup olive oil
2 cloves garlic
1 onion, chopped
2 anchovy fillets, finely chopped
3 sprigs parsley, chopped
2 cups peeled and chopped ripe tomatoes
1/4 cup finely chopped walnuts
1-1/4 cups dry white wine
3 pounds firm fish fillets (cod, halibut, salmon, or
    bass), cut into pieces and boned
1 bay leaf
salt and white pepper to taste
accompaniment: French or Italian bread

Heat oil in a flameproof casserole or Dutch oven
and sauté garlic cloves and onion; discard cloves
when brown. Add anchovies, parsley and tomatoes.
Combine walnuts and wine and add to casserole.
Simmer 15 minutes and add fish, bay leaf, salt and
pepper. Continue cooking for about 15 minutes, or
until fish is just tender. Serve with French or
Italian bread.

PUERTO RICAN SEAFOOD-AND-MEAT STEW

Serves 4 to 6
2 onions, chopped
2 cloves garlic, minced
1 or more fresh green chili peppers, seeded
    and chopped
2 tablespoons lard or olive oil
2 cups rice
1-1/2 quarts chicken stock or water, heated
1 pound firm white fish fillets, cut into
    1-inch cubes
1/2 pound fresh lobster meat, cut into chunks, or
1/2 pound scallops
1/2 pound ham, cut into 1/2-inch chunks
1/4 pound chorizo sausage, sliced 1/2-inch thick
1 bay leaf
garnish:
    chopped coriander
    lemon or lime wedges

Sauté onions, garlic and chili pepper in lard for 2
minutes; then add rice and sauté 5 minutes, or
until rice is shiny. Add half of the stock and cook
over high heat until liquid is absorbed. Lower heat
to medium and add remaining stock. Place fish,
lobster or scallops, ham, chorizo and bay leaf on
top of rice. Cover and cook over low heat for 15
minutes, or until rice is tender. Serve in large
individual bowls, with coriander sprinkled over top
and lemon and lime wedges on the side.

FISH AND VEGETABLE STEW WITH RICE

Serves 4 to 6
1 onion, sliced
2 tablespoons corn oil
2 ripe tomatoes, peeled, seeded and diced
1 or more fresh green chili peppers, seeded and
    diced
2 carrots, sliced
2 small sweet potatoes, peeled and cut into
    1-inch cubes
1/2 pound cabbage, shredded (approximately
    1/2 head)
1/2 pound okra, sliced
2 pounds firm white fish fillets, such as halibut or
    swordfish, cut into 1-1/2-inch pieces
salt and freshly ground pepper to taste
accompaniment: freshly cooked rice

Sauté the onion in oil in a large saucepan until
transparent. Add 1 quart water and the vegetables.
Bring to a rapid boil, cover, lower heat and simmer
40 minutes. Add the fish fillets and simmer for 15
minutes, or until fish is just tender. Season with
salt and pepper. Serve over rice in large soup plates.

OYSTER STEW

Serves 6
1 quart oysters with liquor
2 tablespoons butter
1 quart half-and-half or half milk and half
    heavy cream, scalded
salt and white pepper to taste
paprika and celery salt to taste
accompaniment: oyster crackers

Heat oysters and liquor with the butter until oysters are plump and edges begin to curl. Remove
from heat and combine with half-and-half. Season
with salt and pepper and ladle into warmed soup
bowls. Sprinkle with paprika and celery salt. Serve
with oyster crackers.

SEAFOOD

BOUILLABAISSE

Serves 10 to 12

2 pounds ripe tomatoes, peeled, seeded and
    chopped
4 leeks, chopped
2 onions, chopped
1 carrot, chopped
3 cloves garlic, minced
3 tablespoons chopped parsley
1 bay leaf
1/2 teaspoon dried thyme
1/2 teaspoon saffron threads
1 teaspoon grated orange peel
1/2 cup olive oil
1 cup dry white wine
2 to 3 pounds fresh lobster or crab, cut up in
    their shells
3 pounds assorted firm fresh fish fillets, such as
    red snapper, cod, halibut, perch, bass or
    mackerel, cut into 1-inch slices
12 clams or mussels in shells, well scrubbed
salt and freshly ground pepper to taste
sliced French bread
accompaniment: French bread and sweet butter

Combine all the vegetables and seasonings in a large
soup kettle with olive oil, wine and 2 quarts water.
Bring to a rapid boil, then add lobster or crab and
cook for 8 minutes, covered. Add remaining seafood, cover and cook 8 to 10 minutes more; do not
overcook. Remove seafood to a warm serving dish;
put a slice of French bread on the bottom of each
soup bowl and pour broth over it. Serve soup and
seafood separately with additional French bread
and sweet butter on the side.

SHRIMP AND VEGETABLE STIR-FRY

Following directions for Beef and Vegetable Stir-
Fry, page 114, substitute 1 pound medium-sized
shrimp, shelled and deveined, for the beef and use
only 1 tablespoon soy sauce. When stir-frying
shrimp, cook 1 minute before removing to plate.

SAN FRANCISCO OYSTER LOAF

Serves 4 to 6
1 long loaf sourdough French bread
1 small eggplant, peeled and finely chopped
1 medium-sized onion, finely chopped
1 clove garlic, minced
6 tablespoons butter
1 tablespoon olive oil
salt and freshly ground pepper to taste
1/2 teaspoon dried tarragon
1/4 cup chopped parsley
2 tablespoons dry white wine
1 pint oysters, drained (reserve liquor) and chopped

Prepare the bread by cutting off the top one-third and taking out the center, leaving a shell 3/4 inch thick. Set bread aside. In a skillet sauté eggplant, onion and garlic in butter and oil. Season with salt, pepper, tarragon and parsley and cook over low heat about 15 minutes, stirring occasionally. The vegetables should be limp, but not brown. Add the wine and reserved oyster liquor and cook until liquid is reduced by one-half. Add chopped oysters and cook over medium heat 5 minutes. Put the mixture into the bread crust and replace top. Wrap in heavy aluminum foil and bake in preheated 400° oven for 20 minutes. Unwrap, slice, and serve on a warmed platter.

NEW ORLEANS OYSTER LOAF

Serves 4
4 small French bread rolls
melted butter
1 pint oysters, well drained
4 tablespoons butter
salt and freshly ground pepper to taste
Tabasco sauce to taste

Cut tops off French rolls and scoop out most of the center. Brush the cut side of the tops and center with melted butter. Place rolls and tops in a preheated 425° oven to toast lightly. While rolls are toasting, sauté the oysters in 4 tablespoons butter until the edges curl, about 2 or 3 minutes. Season with salt, pepper and Tabasco. Fill the hot rolls with the oysters, replace tops and serve.

SEAFOOD

CREAMED CODFISH ON TOAST

Serves 4
1 pound salt cod
1 cup heavy cream
1 cup milk
pinch of cayenne pepper
1 teaspoon flour
3 tablespoons butter, at room temperature
4 thick slices of freshly buttered, hot toast
freshly grated nutmeg
3 hard-cooked eggs, chopped
2 tablespoons chopped parsley

Soak the cod overnight in water to cover. Drain, rinse and put in a skillet with fresh water to cover. Bring to a boil and simmer for 10 minutes. Drain and pat dry with paper toweling. Cut in small pieces. Heat the cream and milk in the skillet and add the cod. Simmer for 5 minutes and add the cayenne pepper. Mix the flour and butter into a paste and gradually add to the creamed cod mixture, stirring until thickened. Spoon over the toast. Dust with nutmeg and sprinkle with the chopped eggs and parsley.

CODFISH, POTATO AND ONION SAUTÉ

Serves 4
1 pound salt cod
2 potatoes, peeled and thinly sliced
2 onions, thinly sliced
3 tablespoons each butter and corn oil
2 cloves garlic, minced
1/2 teaspoon freshly ground pepper
malt vinegar (or any mild vinegar)
chopped parsley

Soak codfish overnight in water to cover. Drain, rinse and put in a skillet with fresh water to cover. Bring to a boil and simmer 10 minutes. Drain and pat dry with paper toweling. Cut fish into small pieces. Set aside. Heat the skillet and sauté the potatoes and onions in the butter and oil for 10 minutes. Add the garlic and return the fish to the skillet, cooking 10 minutes over high heat, or until the fish, potatoes and onions turn golden brown. Season with pepper. Sprinkle with vinegar and parsley.

SEAFOOD

FISH CURRY

Serves 6 to 8
1 teaspoon coriander seeds
1/2 teaspoon fennel seeds
1/4 teaspoon cumin seeds
1 small stick cinnamon
2 cardamom seeds
3 peppercorns
1/4 teaspoon cayenne pepper
1/2 teaspoon ground turmeric
2 tablespoons each butter and corn oil
2 thin slices ginger root, minced, or
1/2 teaspoon ground ginger
1 small onion, sliced
2 cups coconut milk, page 24
2 pounds firm white fish fillets (halibut, cod or
    bass) cut into 1/2-inch by 1-inch strips
accompaniment: freshly cooked rice

Grind together coriander, fennel, cumin, cinnamon, cardamom and peppercorns; set aside. In a skillet sauté the cayenne pepper and turmeric in the butter and oil. Add ground spices, ginger and onion and continue sautéing until onion is transparent. Add coconut milk and fish and simmer 10 minutes, or until fish is tender. Serve over rice.

POACHED FISH LOAF

Serves 6 to 8
2 pounds fresh ground fish, preferably a mixture
    of a variety of fish such as flounder, eel, carp
    and halibut
1/4 cup capers
3 tablespoons butter, at room temperature
1/2 teaspoon dried tarragon
1/4 teaspoon dried rosemary
1 teaspoon salt
1/2 teaspoon white pepper
2 cups dry white wine
2 cups water
1 onion, quartered
2 whole cloves
2 celery ribs with leaves, quartered
3 sprigs parsley
accompaniments: melted butter, prepared
    mustard, thinly sliced sweet red onions,
    lemon wedges, rye bread

Combine ground fish, capers, butter, tarragon, rosemary, salt and pepper and form into a loaf. Place on a double thickness of wet cheesecloth. Wrap roll and tie at both ends with white string; set aside. Put the remaining ingredients in a large pot. Bring to a rapid boil, lower heat and put the fish loaf in the pan. Cover and simmer gently for 40 minutes. Remove fish loaf; let rest 10 minutes and unwrap carefully. Serve with accompaniments. This dish may also be served chilled.

TEMPURA

Serves 6

1 pound large shrimp
1 pound firm white fish fillets (flounder, halibut or bass), cut into small pieces
any combination of the following vegetables:
   1 carrot, sliced diagonally into 1/8-inch-thick slices
   1 sweet potato, peeled and sliced diagonally into 1/8-inch-thick slices
   12 green beans, trimmed but left whole
   12 asparagus, trimmed but left whole
   1 small onion, quartered and separated
   1 small eggplant, halved and cut into 1/4-inch slices
3 cups corn oil

Batter

2 eggs
2 cups cold water
2-1/2 cups sifted cake flour

Dashi Sauce

2 cups dashi*
1/2 cup Japanese soy sauce
2 tablespoons mirin (Japanese sweet rice wine) or sherry

accompaniments:
   freshly grated ginger root and daikon (radish)
   freshly cooked rice

Combine ingredients for Dashi Sauce and pour into individual dipping bowls. Set aside.

Insert point of small knife under the shell of each shrimp cutting from head to tail (but not through tail segment). Peel shrimp carefully, leaving tail intact. Score underside of shrimp in 3 places so that it will flatten when cooked. Prepare white fish and vegetables as directed and set aside. Heat corn oil in a skillet until temperature measures 330° or until a drop of batter sizzles.

To make batter, mix eggs with water. Stir in flour lightly. (Some flour will remain floating on top.) Do not overstir; batter should be lumpy. Dip individual pieces of seafood and vegetables into batter and deep fry for 30 to 60 seconds, or until just lightly golden. Remove to a paper towel. Serve each person an assortment of seafood and vegetables with a bowl of Dashi Sauce. Ginger and daikon may be added to the sauce as desired. Serve with freshly cooked rice.

*Japanese soup stock; instant variety is available in Japanese markets.

SEAFOOD

SHRIMP JAMBALAYA

Serves 6 to 8
1 onion, chopped
2 cloves garlic, minced
3 tablespoons peanut oil
1 bell pepper, diced
2 cups peeled and chopped ripe tomatoes
1/4 teaspoon cayenne pepper
1/4 teaspoon dried thyme
1/4 teaspoon ground cloves
salt and freshly ground pepper
1 pound raw ham, cut into 1/2-inch dice
2 cups rice
1 pound medium-sized shrimp, shelled
   and deveined
garnish: chopped parsley

Sauté onion and garlic in oil in a large skillet for 5 minutes. Add bell pepper, tomatoes, cayenne, thyme, cloves, salt, pepper and 3 cups water. Bring to a boil and add ham and rice. Cover, lower heat to simmer and cook 20 minutes. Place shrimp on top, cover and cook another 10 minutes. Serve garnished with chopped parsley.

SHRIMP IN COCONUT SAUCE

Serves 4
1 yellow onion, chopped
2 green onions, chopped
2 tablespoons each butter and corn oil
1 pound medium-sized shrimp,
   shelled and deveined
1 bell pepper, cut into strips
2 cups peeled and diced ripe tomatoes
1/2 cup slivered blanched almonds
1 tablespoon minced basil
1 teaspoon salt
1/4 teaspoon white pepper
1 tablespoon cornstarch
1 cup coconut milk, page 24
accompaniment: freshly cooked rice

Sauté yellow and green onions in butter and oil for 3 minutes. Add remaining ingredients, except cornstarch and coconut milk, and cook for 3 minutes. Make a paste by stirring cornstarch into some of the coconut milk; add remaining coconut milk and blend until smooth. Blend milk with shrimp mixture and heat through. Serve over rice.

SWORDFISH, HAM AND POTATO CASSEROLE

Serves 6

4 to 6 potatoes, peeled and thinly sliced
1 large onion, sliced
salt and freshly ground pepper to taste
1-1/2 pounds swordfish steaks, cut 3/4-inch thick
1/4 cup corn oil
1 clove garlic, minced
1/4 cup chopped parsley
1 fresh green chili pepper, seeded and
   finely chopped
1/2 pound smoked ham, thinly sliced
1 cup grated mozzarella cheese

Oil a 9- by 13-inch baking dish and make layers of half the potato and onion slices; season with salt and pepper and place swordfish steaks on top. Drizzle with half the oil. Scatter garlic, parsley and chili pepper on top. Add layer of sliced ham and cover with remaining potato and onion slices. Season with salt and pepper, drizzle with remaining oil and top with grated cheese. Bake in a preheated 375° oven for 1 hour, or until potatoes are tender.

FISH PUDDING

Serves 6

1 pound sole fillets (haddock or flounder may
   be substituted)
1 cup coconut milk, page 24
1 teaspoon salt
1 teaspoon ground turmeric
1 clove garlic, minced
1/4 teaspoon cayenne pepper
1 tablespoon paprika
1 small onion, minced
5 eggs
garnish: sliced cucumbers
accompaniment: boiled potatoes

Cut fish into 1/2-inch strips and place in a buttered 1-quart casserole. Mix together coconut milk, salt, turmeric, garlic, cayenne, paprika and minced onion, and gradually beat in eggs, one at a time. Pour over fish. Place casserole in a pan of hot water and bake in a preheated 325° oven for 50 minutes, or until knife inserted in center comes out clean. Serve at once, garnished with cucumbers and accompanied with boiled potatoes.

SEAFOOD

FISH AND RICE CASSEROLE

Serves 3 or 4
1 pound white fish fillets (cod, halibut or sole)
4 tablespoons butter
1 onion, chopped
1/2 cup pine nuts
1 cup rice
2 cups fish stock or water
salt and white pepper to taste
1 cup fresh peas (1 pound, unshelled)

Brown fish in 2 tablespoons of the butter in a flameproof 2-quart casserole; remove fish from casserole and set aside. Sauté onion and pine nuts in remaining 2 tablespoons of butter in the casserole for 2 minutes. Add rice and continue sautéing until rice is shiny, about 5 minutes. Pour in stock, add salt and pepper and place browned fish fillets and peas on top. Cover and place in a preheated 350° oven for 45 minutes or until rice is tender.

KEDGEREE
(Curried Baked Fish and Rice)

Serves 4
3 cups cooked rice
2 cups cooked, flaked white fish (flounder, sole, halibut or bass)
1 cup grated mild Cheddar cheese
3 eggs, lightly beaten
3 tablespoons chopped green onion
2 teaspoons curry powder
1/4 teaspoon Worcestershire sauce
pinch of cayenne pepper
salt and freshly ground pepper to taste
3 tablespoons butter
accompaniments: banana slices, chopped cucumber, chutney, chopped roasted peanuts

Combine all the ingredients, except the butter, and pour into a buttered 1-1/2-quart baking dish. Dot with butter and bake in a preheated 350° oven for 35 to 40 minutes, or until golden brown. Serve with accompaniments.

BAKED AVOCADO WITH CRAB

Serves 6
3 firm unpeeled avocados, halved and pitted
juice of 1 lemon
1-1/2 cups flaked cooked crab meat
2 tablespoons chopped chives
1 tablespoon capers
1 cup White Sauce, following
pinch of cayenne pepper
salt and white pepper to taste
1/2 cup grated Cheddar cheese
2 tablespoons bread crumbs
accompaniment: crusty French bread rolls

Sprinkle cut avocados with lemon juice. Combine crab meat, chives, capers, White Sauce, cayenne, salt and pepper and fill avocados with mixture. Mix together the cheese and bread crumbs and sprinkle over the crab filling. Place the stuffed avocados in a shallow baking dish with 1/2-inch hot water and bake in a preheated 350° oven for 25 minutes. Serve with crusty rolls.

Variation Substitute for the crab meat, small cooked shrimp, cooked flaked salmon or tuna, cooked diced chicken or turkey.

WHITE SAUCE

Makes 1 cup
2 tablespoons butter
2 tablespoons flour
1 cup milk
salt
white pepper
2 tablespoons heavy cream (optional)

In a saucepan melt butter over low heat and stir in the flour. Cook for 3 minutes. Do not brown. Stir in milk and continue cooking over low heat, stirring constantly, until sauce begins to thicken. Season with salt and pepper. For a richer white sauce, the heavy cream may be added before completion.

POULTRY

CHICKEN FRICASSEE WITH RICE

Serves 4
1 3 1/2- to 4-pound fryer chicken, cut up
2 tablespoons each butter and corn oil
1 onion, chopped
salt and white pepper to taste
1/2 teaspoon dried tarragon
2-1/2 cups chicken stock
1 cup rice
1/4 pound small button mushrooms
6 to 8 small boiling onions
1 carrot, thinly sliced
1 cup fresh peas (1 pound, unshelled)
1 cup heavy cream
3 egg yolks
garnish: chopped parsley

Top-of-the-Stove Method
In a Dutch oven sauté the chicken over medium heat in butter and oil, browning on all sides, about 10 minutes. Add chopped onion, salt, pepper, tar-ragon and chicken stock. Cover and simmer for 20 minutes. Stir in rice, mushrooms, boiling onions and carrot and continue cooking over low heat for 15 minutes. Add the peas, cover and simmer 10 minutes longer. Remove pot from heat and blend cream and egg yolks gradually into chicken and rice mixture. Return to low heat and heat through. Garnish with parsley and serve.

Wet Clay Cooker Method
Combine chopped onion, salt, pepper, tarragon and only 2 cups chicken stock in a pre-soaked unglazed clay cooker. Stir in rice, mushrooms, boiling onions and carrot. Top with chicken pieces and drizzle with melted butter and oil. Cover and place in a cold oven. Turn oven to 400° and bake 1 hour and 15 minutes. Remove from oven, blend cream and egg yolks gradually into chicken and rice mixture and add peas. Cover and return to oven for 10 minutes. Remove from oven and let stand 10 minutes. Garnish with parsley and serve.

POULTRY

CHICKEN RAGOUT

Serves 3 to 4
2 tablespoons corn oil
1 onion, chopped
1 3-pound fryer chicken, cut up, with giblets
2 tablespoons chopped parsley
1 teaspoon ground cumin
2 cups chicken stock
2 potatoes, peeled and diced
1/4 cup fresh lemon juice
1 egg, beaten
2 tablespoons chopped dill

Top-of-the-Stove Method (Dutch oven, flameproof casserole or large skillet may be used)
Heat oil and sauté onion until transparent. Add chicken parts and giblets and brown on all sides. Add parsley, cumin and stock; cover and simmer for 30 minutes. Add potatoes and cook 20 minutes or until tender. Stir in lemon juice. Take 1/2 cup of cooking liquid from pot and stir in beaten egg; return egg mixture to pot and stir constantly until thickened. Do not allow liquid to come to a boil. Stir in fresh dill just before serving.

Slow Cooker Method
Brown chicken and giblets with onion in oil in a skillet or slow cooker with a browning unit. Put potatoes in the bottom of the slow cooker and place browned chicken and onion on top. Add parsley, cumin and 1-1/2 cups stock; cover and cook on low for 6 to 8 hours. When ready to serve, stir in lemon juice. Take 1/2 cup of cooking liquid from pot and stir beaten egg into it; return egg mixture to pot and turn on high. Stirring constantly, cook until thickened. Do not allow liquid to come to a boil. Stir in fresh dill just before serving.

Wet Clay Cooker Method
Combine all ingredients using only 1-1/2 cups stock (browning is not necessary), except lemon juice, egg and dill in a pre-soaked unglazed clay cooker. Cover and place in a cold oven. Turn oven to 400° and bake 1 hour and 15 minutes. Remove from oven, uncover and stir in lemon juice. Take 1/2 cup of cooking liquid and stir beaten egg into it. Stir egg mixture into pot. Cover and let stand 10 minutes. Stir in fresh dill just before serving.

CHICKEN STEW, ITALIAN STYLE

Serves 4

1 3-1/2- to 4-pound chicken, cut up (or equiva-
   lent weight of chicken parts)
3 tablespoons olive oil
2 onions, sliced
1 teaspoon salt
1/2 teaspoon freshly ground pepper
1 celery rib, cut into small chunks
2 cups diced potatoes
1 cup peeled and chopped ripe tomatoes
1 teaspoon dried oregano
3 tablespoons chopped parsley
1 cup fresh peas (1 pound, unshelled)

Oven Method (Dutch oven, large skillet or heatproof casserole may be used)

Rub the chicken or chicken parts with the olive oil and brown with onions in a preheated 425° oven for 15 minutes. Add other ingredients, except peas, and 1 cup water. Cover the vessel with a tight-fitting lid, lower oven to 325° and continue cooking for 45 minutes. Add the peas and cook an additional 15 minutes.

Slow Cooker Method

Brown the chicken parts in oil in a skillet or a slow cooker with a browning unit. Add salt, pepper and onions and cook for another 5 minutes. Put celery and potatoes in the bottom of the slow cooker and top with browned chicken, onions, tomatoes, 1/2 cup water, oregano and parsley. Cover and cook on low for 6 to 8 hours. Add peas, cover and cook on high 15 minutes.

Pressure Cooker Method

Heat the oil in the pressure cooker and brown the chicken parts. Add salt, pepper, onions, celery, tomatoes, 1 cup water, oregano and parsley. Cover and bring to full pressure. When steam appears, reduce heat and cook on low for 10 minutes. Reduce pressure completely and add potatoes. Continue cooking, covered, 10 minutes, not under pressure. Add peas and cook 5 minutes. Let stand covered 10 to 15 minutes to blend flavors.

POULTRY

BRUNSWICK STEW

Serves 6
2 slices bacon, diced
3 tablespoons flour
1 teaspoon salt
1/2 teaspoon freshly ground pepper
pinch of cayenne pepper
1 3- to 4-pound rabbit or chicken, cut up, with
   giblets
3 onions, thinly sliced
4 ripe tomatoes, peeled and chopped
1 sweet red pepper, chopped
1/2 teaspoon dried thyme
2 cups fresh lima beans
2 cups freshly grated corn kernels
1/2 pound okra, sliced
2 tablespoons chopped parsley
1 tablespoon Worcestershire sauce

Top-of-the-Stove Method
(Dutch oven or flameproof casserole may be used)
Cook the bacon in its own fat until rendered.
Remove the bacon bits and set aside. Combine
flour, salt, pepper and cayenne and dredge rabbit
or chicken. Brown the pieces in the rendered fat
with the onions. Add 2 cups boiling water, tomatoes, sweet red pepper and thyme. Cover and simmer 1 hour. Add remaining ingredients, including
reserved bacon, cover and continue cooking 15 to
20 minutes or until vegetables are tender.

Slow Cooker Method

Cook the bacon in its own fat until rendered in a skillet or a slow cooker with a browning unit. Remove the bacon bits and set aside. Combine flour, salt, pepper and cayenne and dredge the rabbit or chicken. Brown the pieces in the rendered fat with the onions. Add 1-1/2 cups boiling water, tomatoes, sweet red pepper and thyme to a slow cooker with the meat. Cover and cook on low 6 to 8 hours. Add remaining ingredients including reserved bacon, cover and cook on high 25 minutes or until vegetables are tender.

Pressure Cooker Method

In a pressure cooker cook the bacon in its own fat until rendered. Remove the bacon bits and set aside. Combine flour, salt, pepper and cayenne and dredge rabbit or chicken. Brown the pieces in the rendered fat with the onions. Add 3 cups water, tomatoes, sweet red pepper and thyme. Cover and bring to full pressure. When steam appears, reduce heat and cook on low 15 minutes. Reduce pressure completely, uncover and add remaining ingredients, including reserved bacon. Cover and cook 10 minutes, not under pressure. Let stand, covered, 10 to 15 minutes to blend flavors.

POULTRY

CHICKEN SAUTÉ, HUNTER'S STYLE

Serves 4 to 6
1 onion, sliced
1 carrot, chopped
1 celery rib, chopped
4 tablespoons butter
1-1/2 tablespoons olive oil
1 3-pound fryer chicken, cut up
1/2 cup dry white wine
2 cups peeled and chopped ripe tomatoes
salt and freshly ground pepper to taste
pinch of ground cinnamon
2 whole cloves
1/2 pound small button mushrooms

In a large skillet or Dutch oven, sauté onion, carrot and celery in butter and oil. Add chicken pieces and brown lightly. Add wine and tomatoes and salt and pepper lightly. Sprinkle with cinnamon and toss in cloves. Continue cooking over medium heat for 45 minutes, or until chicken is tender. Add mushrooms for last 10 minutes of cooking period.

BREAST OF CHICKEN WITH WILD RICE

Serves 6
6 whole chicken breasts, halved and boned
1/4 pound butter
3 tablespoons flour
1/2 teaspoon paprika
1/4 teaspoon salt
dash of freshly ground pepper
1-1/2 cups half-and-half
1/2 cup raisins, plumped in
1/2 cup fresh orange juice
garnish: watercress sprigs
accompaniment: freshly cooked wild rice

Brown chicken on both sides in butter in a skillet. Cover and cook over low heat 30 to 40 minutes, or until chicken is tender. Remove chicken from skillet, place on serving platter and keep warm. Pour off all but 3 tablespoons of the butter and stir in flour, paprika, salt and pepper. Add half-and-half and cook over low heat, stirring constantly, until smooth and thickened. Stir in raisin-orange juice mixture and heat through. Pour sauce over chicken and garnish with watercress. Serve with wild rice.

COUNTRY CAPTAIN

Serves 6
1 3-pound fryer chicken, cut up
3 tablespoons flour
1 teaspoon salt
1/4 teaspoon freshly ground pepper
3 tablespoons each butter and corn oil
1 clove garlic, minced
1 onion, chopped
1 bell pepper, chopped
1-1/2 teaspoons curry powder
2 cups peeled and chopped ripe tomatoes
1/4 cup dried currants
accompaniments:
    freshly cooked rice
    chutney
    blanched toasted almonds
    chopped green onions

Dust the chicken pieces with the flour, salt and pepper. In a large skillet brown the chicken in butter and oil on all sides. Remove from pan and set aside. Add the garlic, onion, pepper and curry powder to the skillet and cook for 3 minutes over low heat. Add the tomatoes and return the chicken pieces, skin side up, to the skillet. Cover and simmer for 30 minutes, or until chicken is tender. Stir in currants. Serve over rice with accompaniments.

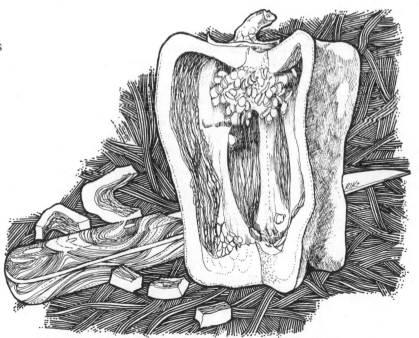

POULTRY

CURRY CHICKEN WITH COCONUT SAUCE

Serves 4
2 onions, sliced
2 cloves garlic, minced
2 tablespoons butter
1 or more tablespoons curry powder
1 teaspoon chili powder
1 teaspoon salt
1-1/2 cups coconut milk, page 24
1 3-pound fryer chicken, cut up
1 pound potatoes, peeled and cut into 1-inch cubes
1/2 cup chopped roasted Virginia peanuts
garnish: chopped coriander, green onions and
    seeded and chopped cucumbers

In a Dutch oven sauté the onions and garlic in the butter until soft. Stir in curry and chili powders and salt. Add 1 cup of the coconut milk, the chicken and the potatoes. Cover and simmer for 30 minutes, or until chicken is tender. Add the remaining coconut milk and peanuts and simmer 10 minutes longer. Serve with garnishes.

CURRIED CHICKEN

Serves 4
2 large onions, sliced
2 cloves garlic, minced
4 tablespoons butter
1/4 teaspoon ground ginger
1 teaspoon ground coriander
1/4 teaspoon ground turmeric
1/8 teaspoon cayenne pepper
1 3-pound fryer chicken, cut up
2 tablespoons plain yogurt
1 bay leaf
1 teaspoon salt
1 tablespoon cornstarch, mixed with
3 tablespoons water
accompaniment: freshly cooked rice

In a heavy skillet brown onions and garlic in butter; add 1/2 cup water, ginger, coriander, turmeric and cayenne. Stir well and add chicken, yogurt, bay leaf, salt and 2 more cups water. Cover and simmer until tender, about 35 minutes. Just before serving, blend in cornstarch binder and simmer until sauce is thickened. Serve over rice.

CHICKEN À LA KING

Serves 6
1 cup sliced fresh mushrooms
1 bell pepper, thinly sliced
4 tablespoons butter
2 cups White Sauce, page 51
1/2 cup dry sherry
1-1/2 teaspoons dried tarragon
pinch cayenne pepper
1/2 teaspoon salt
1/4 teaspoon white pepper
4 egg yolks
1/2 cup heavy cream
3 cups cubed cooked chicken
2 tablespoons chopped pimiento
accompaniment: freshly cooked rice,
    toast triangles or patty shells

In a saucepan sauté mushrooms and bell pepper in the butter for 5 minutes. Add White Sauce, sherry, tarragon, cayenne and salt and pepper. Bring just to a boil, stirring constantly. Combine egg yolks with cream and stir into the sauce. Add the chicken and heat through without boiling. Sprinkle with pimiento and serve over rice, toast or patty shells.

Variation Substitute turkey for the chicken.

CHICKEN AND RICE, PERUVIAN STYLE

Serves 4 to 6
1/4 pound lean salt pork, diced and blanched
3 tablespoons olive oil
1 3-1/2- to 4-pound fryer chicken, cut up
1 onion, sliced
1 green bell pepper, sliced
1 sweet red pepper, sliced
2 cloves garlic, minced
1 cup peeled and chopped ripe tomatoes
1 or more fresh jalapeño chilies, seeded and diced
1/2 teaspoon powdered saffron
1 quart chicken stock (or half stock and half water)
1 bay leaf
1-1/2 cups rice
1 pound chorizo sausages, sliced 1/2 inch thick

Heat a Dutch oven or large skillet and sauté the salt pork in oil for 2 minutes. Add the chicken and continue to sauté, turning often to lightly brown all sides, about 10 minutes. Add the onion, peppers and garlic and sauté 2 more minutes. Add tomatoes, chilies, saffron, stock and bay leaf. Bring to boil, cover and simmer 15 minutes. Add the rice and chorizos. Bring to a boil again, cover and simmer for 20 minutes, or until rice is tender.

POULTRY

ARROZ CON POLLO, HONDURAN STYLE

Serves 4 to 6
1 2-1/2- to 3-pound fryer chicken, cut up
1 teaspoon salt
1/4 cup olive oil
1 onion, sliced
1 clove garlic, minced
1 teaspoon caraway seeds
1/4 cup tomato paste
1 cup rice
1 cup pitted black olives
1 cup peas (1 pound, unshelled)
1 cup light beer
2 cups shredded cabbage
1/4 cup capers

Rub chicken pieces with salt. In a Dutch oven or heavy skillet, brown chicken in hot oil on all sides. Add the onion, garlic, caraway seeds, tomato paste and 2 cups water. Bring to a rapid boil, lower heat, cover and simmer 30 minutes. Add remaining ingredients and cover and simmer an additional 30 minutes.

CHICKEN PILAU

Serves 4 to 6
1 3-1/2-pound fryer chicken, cut up
salt and freshly ground pepper to taste
1 onion, chopped
3 celery ribs, chopped
1/2 cup raisins
6 tablespoons butter, or
3 tablespoons each butter and corn oil
1-1/2 cups long-grain rice
1 cup peeled and chopped ripe tomatoes
2 tablespoons minced parsley
1 teaspoon dried thyme
3 cups chicken stock (or half stock and half water)
garnish: watercress sprigs

Rub chicken pieces with salt and pepper; set aside. Sauté the onion, celery and raisins in butter in a large skillet or flameproof casserole until they are soft. Add rice and sauté until rice grains appear translucent; then blend in tomatoes, parsley and thyme. Place chicken pieces on top of rice, add chicken stock and bring to a rapid boil. Lower heat to simmer, cover and cook for 30 minutes, or until chicken is tender and rice has absorbed the liquid. Serve garnished with watercress sprigs.

BRAISED RABBIT WITH POTATOES, ONIONS AND PEAS

Serves 4

1 3-pound rabbit, cut up
2 tablespoons flour
3 tablespoons each butter and olive oil
12 small boiling onions
8 small new potatoes
1 teaspoon salt
1/2 teaspoon freshly ground pepper
1 celery rib, cut up
1 bay leaf
2 cloves garlic
1/2 teaspoon dried thyme
1 cup chicken stock
1/2 cup dry white wine
1 cup fresh peas (1 pound, unshelled)
garnish: chopped parsley

Top-of-the-Stove Method
(Dutch oven or flameproof casserole may be used)
Sprinkle the rabbit pieces with flour. Brown rabbit pieces in the butter and oil until golden brown. Add all the remaining ingredients except peas. Bring to a boil, cover and simmer 40 minutes, or until rabbit is tender. Add peas and continue simmering for 10 minutes. Sprinkle with parsley.

Wet Clay Cooker Method
Sprinkle the rabbit pieces with flour. Combine the remaining ingredients, except butter and oil and peas, in a pre-soaked unglazed clay cooker. Place rabbit pieces on top and drizzle with melted butter and oil. Cover and place in a cold oven. Turn oven to 400° and bake 1 hour and 15 minutes. Remove from oven, add peas, cover and bake 10 minutes. Remove from oven and let stand 10 minutes. Garnish with parsley.

POULTRY

PAELLA

Serves 6 to 8

1 2-1/2- to 3-pound fryer chicken,
   cut up, with giblets
salt and freshly ground pepper
1/2 cup olive oil
1/2 pound chorizo sausages, blanched and
   cut into 1/2-inch slices
1 small onion, chopped
2 cloves garlic, minced

1 red or green bell pepper, cut into
   1/4-inch wide strips
3 cups long-grain rice
1 cup peeled, seeded and chopped tomatoes
1/2 teaspoon saffron threads, dissolved in
1/2 cup hot water
1/2 pound medium-sized shrimp, shelled and
   deveined with tails intact
6 or more clams in shells, well scrubbed
6 or more mussels in shells, well scrubbed
1 cup fresh peas or asparagus tips, or
   cut-up green beans
garnish: lemon wedges

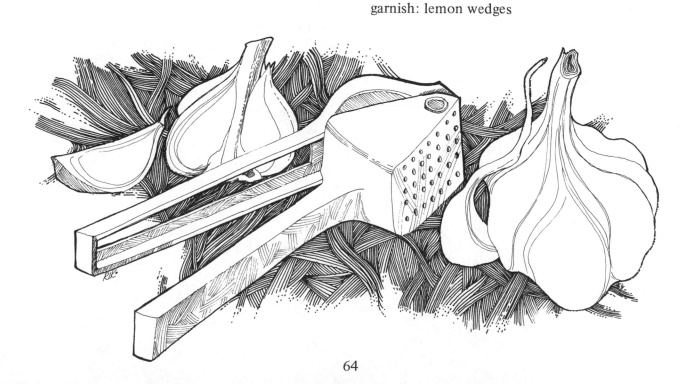

Rub chicken pieces and giblets with salt and pepper. In a paella pan or large skillet, brown seasoned chicken on all sides in 1/4 cup of the olive oil. Remove from pan and set aside. Add chorizo slices to pan, brown and remove. Add remaining oil to pan and sauté onion, garlic, pepper and rice for 5 minutes. Add tomatoes and cook until liquid has evaporated, stirring frequently. Blend in saffron and water and pour 2 cups of boiling water over all. Cook over high heat until rice has absorbed water. Pour 2 more cups of boiling water over rice and cook until absorbed. Remove from heat, add

chicken pieces and pour 2 more cups of boiling water over all, placing shrimp, clams, mussels and peas on top. Place pan in a preheated 400° oven for 20 minutes. Adjust seasonings with salt and pepper and serve, garnished with lemon wedges, directly from the pan.

Variations One or more of the following ingredients may be added to paella in substitution for any of the above: lobster, squid, eel, firm fish fillets, rabbit, sweetbreads, veal kidneys, other fowl.

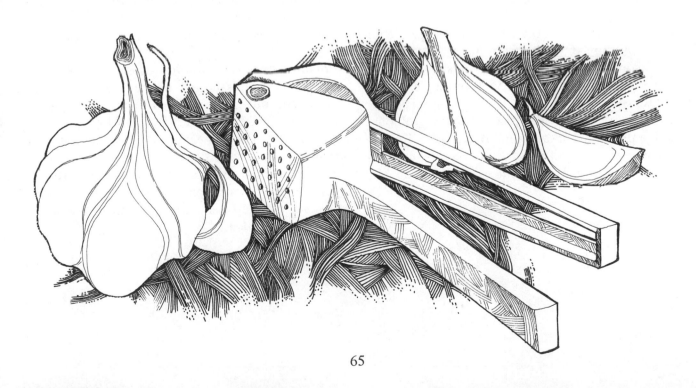

POULTRY

ROAST CHICKEN AND VEGETABLES

Serves 4 to 6
4 tablespoons butter, at room temperature
2 cloves garlic, minced
1 teaspoon salt
1/2 teaspoon freshly ground pepper
1 4-pound roasting chicken
4 sprigs parsley
8 small new potatoes
2 onions, quartered
6 small summer squash
2 celery ribs, cut into 2-inch lengths

Combine the butter, garlic, salt and pepper. Rub half the mixture into the cavity of the chicken and the remainder outside. Put the parsley into the cavity and place the chicken in a roasting pan on a rack. Roast in a preheated 400° oven for 15 minutes. Lower heat to 325°, add potatoes, onions, squash and celery and continue roasting for 1 hour. Baste the chicken and vegetables occasionally with the pan drippings. If the pan is too dry, add 1/2 cup water.

ROAST CHICKEN WITH APRICOTS

Serves 4 to 6
4 tablespoons butter, at room temperature
6 tablespoons honey
1 teaspoon rose water or orange water
1/2 teaspoon freshly grated nutmeg
1 teaspoon salt
1/2 teaspoon freshly ground pepper
1 4-pound roasting chicken
1 pound fresh apricots, pitted and halved
1 tablespoon sugar
1/2 cup toasted slivered almonds or
    chopped pistachios
accompaniment: hot buttered rice or bulgur

Combine butter, 4 tablespoons of the honey, rose water, nutmeg, salt and pepper and rub chicken inside and out. Place chicken in a roasting pan and roast in a preheated 425° oven until golden, about 45 minutes. Lower heat to 350° and add apricots, remaining honey and sugar to pan juices. Continue roasting for 20 minutes, or until tender. Remove chicken to a warm platter, pour pan juices and apricots over chicken, sprinkle with nuts and serve with rice or bulgur.

ROAST CHICKEN
STUFFED WITH EGGPLANT

Serves 6
1 5-pound roasting chicken
2 tablespoons olive oil
salt and freshly ground pepper to taste
1 eggplant, diced
1 onion, chopped
1 bell pepper, diced
2 tomatoes, peeled and chopped
3 cloves garlic, sliced
1/2 teaspoon dried oregano
1 teaspoon salt
1/2 teaspoon freshly ground pepper

Rub the whole chicken, including cavity, with olive oil; sprinkle inside and out with salt and pepper. Combine the remaining ingredients and stuff the chicken. Truss or sew up opening. Place in a roasting pan in a preheated 325° oven for 1-1/2 to 2 hours, or until chicken is tender. The skin should be nicely browned and crisp. Baste with pan juices occasionally during the roasting period.

Note Pan-browned potatoes may be served with the dish; add as many peeled potatoes as desired to the pan and let bake throughout the roasting period.

POULTRY

CUBAN CHICKEN AND CORN PIE

Serves 6 to 8
3 tablespoons butter
4 eggs, beaten
4 cups freshly grated corn kernels, or
1 1-pound can cream-style corn
1/2 pound Monterey Jack cheese, grated
3 cups diced cooked chicken
1 cup diced cooked carrots
1 cup fresh peas (1 pound, unshelled)
1 cup julienne-cut green beans
1/2 cup pitted black olives, sliced
1 cup chicken stock
2 tablespoons raisins
1/2 cup diced green bell pepper
1/2 cup diced sweet red pepper
salt and freshly ground pepper to taste

Butter a 2-quart shallow baking dish with 1 table-spoon of the butter. Combine the eggs, corn and cheese in a bowl. In another bowl, combine all the remaining ingredients except the butter. Layer half the corn mixture in the baking dish and spread vegetable-chicken mixture on top. Top with remaining corn mixture. Dot with the remaining butter and bake in a preheated 350° oven for 1 hour.

STUFFED PERSIAN MELON

Serves 4
1 Persian melon or large cantaloupe
3 tablespoons butter
1 onion, chopped
1/2 pound ground chicken or lamb
2 cups cooked rice or bulgur
1/2 cup chopped walnuts
1/2 cup chopped dried apricots
1/4 cup honey
1/4 teaspoon ground cinnamon
salt and freshly ground pepper to taste
2 tablespoons sugar

Cut a 1-inch top from melon and reserve for a lid. Discard seeds. Scoop out 1 cup of melon pulp, chop and reserve. Heat butter in a flameproof casserole and sauté onion until limp. Add meat and brown lightly. Blend in rice or bulgur, nuts, apricots and melon pulp. Combine honey, 1 cup hot water and cinnamon. Stir into meat mixture and cook until liquid is absorbed. Season with salt and pepper, remove from heat and cool until lukewarm. Sprinkle inside of melon with sugar, stuff with meat-rice mixture and place in same casserole; replace top and secure with toothpicks. Bake in a preheated 350° oven for 1 hour, or until melon is tender.

PUMPKIN STUFFED WITH BULGUR AND CHICKEN

Serves 4 to 6

1 medium-sized pumpkin
1 pound boneless chicken, cubed
1 onion, chopped
3 tablespoons butter
1 celery rib, including leaves, chopped
1 apple, peeled, cored and diced
1/4 cup dried currants
1 teaspoon grated orange peel
1 teaspoon salt
1/2 teaspoon freshly ground pepper
1/2 teaspoon ground cinnamon
1/4 teaspoon freshly grated nutmeg
1 cup apple cider
1/2 cup bulgur, soaked in water to cover 15 minutes and drained
salt and freshly ground pepper to taste
1/4 cup slivered toasted almonds

Cut 1 inch from top of pumpkin and set aside for lid. Remove seeds and 2 cups of pumpkin pulp from pumpkin; dice pulp and reserve. In a flame-proof casserole sauté meat and onion in butter for 5 minutes. Add celery, reserved pumpkin pulp, apple, currants, orange peel, salt, pepper, cinnamon and nutmeg. Blend well with meat and cook 2 minutes. Pour cider over all, bring to a boil, lower to simmer and cook, covered, for 20 minutes. Remove mixture from heat, add bulgur, season with salt and pepper and stuff pumpkin shell. Cover with pumpkin top, place back in casserole and bake in a preheated 350° oven for 2 hours, or until pumpkin is tender. Sprinkle slivered almonds over top and serve.

POULTRY

TURKEY, CHEESE AND TOMATO OPEN-FACE

Serves 6
3 tablespoons butter
3 French bread rolls, split
6 slices cooked turkey breast
salt and freshly ground pepper
6 slices mozzarella or Monterey Jack cheese
6 large tomato slices
garnish: chopped basil or parsley

Spread butter on cut side of French rolls. Place a slice of turkey on the cut side of each half. Salt and pepper lightly. Cover each turkey slice with a slice of cheese and a slice of tomato. Place in a shallow baking pan and bake in a preheated 375° oven for 15 minutes, or until cheese has melted. Serve at once, garnished with basil or parsley.

BARLEY CASSEROLE

Serves 4
1/2 pound mushrooms, sliced
1 celery rib, diced
1 onion, diced
4 tablespoons butter
1 pound boneless chicken, diced
1 cup pearl barley
2 cups chicken stock
garnish: chopped parsley

Sauté mushrooms, celery and onion in butter in a skillet or flameproof casserole until lightly browned; add chicken and barley and continue sautéing for 5 minutes. Add chicken stock and bring to a boil. Lower heat, cover and simmer for 30 minutes. Garnish with parsley.

CHICKEN AND VEGETABLE STIR-FRY

Following directions for Beef and Vegetable Stir-Fry, page 114, substitute 1 pound boneless chicken breast meat, cut into thin strips or 1/2-inch dice, for the beef and use only 1 tablespoon soy sauce or oyster sauce. When stir-frying chicken, cook about 2 minutes before removing to plate.

CHICKEN LIVERS, MIDDLE EASTERN STYLE

Serves 4
1 pound chicken livers, halved
2 tablespoons flour, seasoned with
salt and freshly ground pepper to taste
4 tablespoons olive oil
1 onion, chopped
1 clove garlic, minced
1 cup bulgur
1/4 teaspoon ground allspice
2 cups chopped zucchini
1/4 cup dried currants
2 tablespoons chopped mint
2 cups chicken stock
garnish: chopped coriander or parsley

Dredge chicken livers with the seasoned flour. Heat a skillet and sauté livers lightly in half the oil. Remove livers to a plate and set aside. In same pan, add remaining oil and sauté onion and garlic until transparent. Add bulgur and continue to sauté until bulgur is shiny, about 2 minutes. Add remaining ingredients and bring to a rapid boil. Lower heat to medium and continue to cook, uncovered, until all liquid is absorbed. Reduce heat to simmer, cover and cook 15 minutes. Place reserved livers on top of bulgur mixture, cover and continue to simmer 5 to 7 minutes to heat through. Serve immediately, garnished with coriander or parsley.

CHICKEN LIVERS PAPRIKA

Serves 4
2 onions, sliced
3 tablespoons corn oil or butter
1 pound chicken livers, halved and sprinkled with
1 tablespoon flour
1 small bell pepper, chopped
2 tomatoes, peeled and chopped
1 tablespoon paprika
salt and freshly ground pepper to taste
1 cup (1/2 pint) sour cream
accompaniment: buttered noodles or freshly
    cooked rice

Sauté the onions in 2 tablespoons of the oil in a skillet until transparent. Add the livers and sauté for 5 minutes; remove onions and livers from skillet and set aside. Add remaining oil to pan; add pepper and tomatoes and cook over medium heat for 10 minutes. Add paprika, salt and pepper. Return chicken livers and onions to skillet and cook for 10 minutes. Stir in sour cream and serve over noodles or rice.

LAMB

MEDITERRANEAN LAMB STEW

Serves 6 to 8

2 pounds boneless lamb, cut into 1-inch cubes
1 cup long-grain rice
1 pound potatoes, peeled and sliced
2 onions, sliced
1 teaspoon salt
1/2 teaspoon freshly ground pepper
1 teaspoon ground cumin
1 pound zucchini, sliced
1 12-ounce package frozen artichoke hearts,
    thawed and halved
2 cups peeled and diced ripe tomatoes

Oven Method
Layer about one-third of all ingredients listed in order above in a 3-quart casserole. Repeat layers twice. Add just enough water to cover. Cover and bake in a preheated 350° oven for 2 hours, or until lamb is tender. Add water if necessary during the cooking. When done, all the water should be absorbed.

Slow Cooker Method
Place sliced potatoes in the bottom of a slow cooker. Layer remaining ingredients on top as directed in oven method. Pour 2 cups of water over all. Cover and cook on low 8 to 10 hours.

73

LAMB

IRISH LAMB STEW

Serves 6 to 8

2-1/2 pounds boneless lamb, cut into 1-1/2-inch
 cubes
2 tablespoons corn oil
1-1/2 teaspoons salt
1/2 teaspoon freshly ground pepper
4 turnips, cut into 1/2-inch-thick slices
4 carrots, cut diagonally into 1/2-inch-thick slices
2 onions, sliced
4 potatoes, peeled and quartered
2 tablespoons flour
2 tablespoons chopped parsley

Top-of-the-Stove Method
(Dutch oven or large saucepan may be used)
Brown lamb on all sides in oil. Sprinkle with salt
and pepper. Add 3 cups water, bring to boil, reduce heat and simmer, covered, for 1 hour. Add
vegetables to pot and bring to a boil again; reduce
heat and simmer, covered, for 30 minutes, or until
meat and vegetables are tender. Blend flour with
1/4 cup water until it forms a paste; slowly add to
the stew, stirring constantly until slightly thickened. Stir in parsley and serve.

Slow Cooker Method
Brown the meat in oil in a skillet or a slow cooker
with a browning unit. Put all ingredients except
flour and parsley in a slow cooker with the meat.
Add 2 cups water and cook on low, covered, for 8
to 10 hours. Uncover and turn on high. Blend flour
with 1/4 cup water until it forms a paste; slowly
add to the stew, stirring constantly until slightly
thickened. Stir in parsley and serve.

LAMB AND OKRA STEW

Pressure Cooker Method

Brown meat in oil in a pressure cooker. Add 3 cups water, cover and bring to full pressure. When steam appears, reduce heat and cook on low 15 minutes. Reduce pressure completely, add salt, pepper, turnips, carrots, onions and potatoes, cover and simmer, not under pressure, 30 minutes. Blend flour with 1/4 cup water until it forms a paste; slowly add to the stew, stirring constantly until slightly thickened. Stir in parsley and serve.

Wet Clay Cooker Method

Combine all ingredients except flour and parsley, in a pre-soaked unglazed clay cooker. Add 2 cups water, cover and place in a cold oven. Turn oven to 400° and bake 1-1/2 hours. Remove from oven. Blend flour with 1/4 cup water until it forms a paste; slowly add to the stew, stirring constantly until slightly thickened. Cover and let stand 10 minutes. Stir in parsley and serve.

Serves 6 to 8
2 pounds boneless lamb, cut into 1-inch cubes
2 tablespoons corn oil
1 onion, chopped
2 tablespoons flour
1 6-ounce can tomato paste
1 bell pepper, cut into strips
1 teaspoon salt
1/2 teaspoon freshly ground pepper
1 pound okra, cut into 1/2-inch-thick slices
accompaniment: freshly cooked rice or
    French bread

Brown lamb in oil in a Dutch oven. Add onion and flour and brown. Add tomato paste, pepper strips, salt, pepper and 3 cups water. Simmer covered for 1-1/2 hours. Add okra and cook just until tender. Serve with freshly cooked rice or French bread.

LAMB

STUFFED LEG OF LAMB

Serves 6 to 8
1 5-pound leg of lamb, boned
1 teaspoon salt
1 teaspoon freshly ground pepper
1/4 cup raisins
1/4 cup chopped pitted dates
1/4 cup each chopped dried figs and dried apricots
1/4 cup pine nuts
1 small onion, chopped
3/4 cup bulgur, soaked in water to cover
    15 minutes and drained
2 tablespoons chopped parsley or coriander
accompaniment: spinach salad with vinaigrette
    dressing

Rub leg of lamb with salt and pepper. Combine all the remaining ingredients and stuff lamb with mixture; fasten with skewers. Roast on a rack in a roasting pan in a preheated 325° oven for about 2 hours or until done. Baste occasionally with pan juices. Serve with a spinach salad with vinaigrette dressing, if desired.

BOILED LEG OF LAMB

Serves 8
3 cloves garlic, cut in slivers
1 6-pound leg of lamb
6 peppercorns
2 bay leaves
2 sprigs parsley
1 tablespoon salt
4 celery ribs, cut into 4-inch lengths with
    some leaves
8 carrots, halved
4 turnips, halved
8 small onions
1 medium-sized cabbage, cut in 8 wedges
8 new potatoes

Insert garlic slivers with a sharply pointed, narrow knife into various parts of leg. Wrap leg in 2 thicknesses of cheesecloth and tie with white string. Place the lamb in a large pot and cover with cold water. Bring to a boil, skimming off any surface scum, and add peppercorns, bay leaves, parsley and salt. Lower heat, cover and simmer 45 minutes. Add remaining vegetables and cover and simmer 45 minutes longer. Remove leg of lamb from pot and unwrap it; place on warm platter. Remove vegetables from broth and surround lamb with them. Strain broth and serve in cups.

STUFFED CROWN ROAST OF LAMB

Serves 8
1 5- to 6-pound crown roast of lamb
1 pound ground lamb
1 onion, chopped
1 tablespoon olive oil
1 teaspoon salt
1/2 teaspoon freshly ground pepper
1/4 teaspoon each ground cinnamon, cardamom,
　　ginger and cloves
3 cups cooked rice or bulgur
1/2 cup raisins
1/2 cup chopped toasted almonds
garnish:
　　watercress sprigs
　　orange slices

Have butcher prepare crown roast for stuffing. In a skillet brown ground lamb and onion in oil about 5 minutes. Remove from heat and combine with spices, rice, raisins and almonds and stuff crown roast with this mixture. Place roast in a roasting pan, cover top of roast and stuffing with foil and bake in a preheated 325° oven for 2 hours or until lamb is done. Remove foil during last 15 minutes of roasting to brown top. Garnish with watercress and orange slices and serve.

LEG OF LAMB WITH HERBS AND VEGETABLES

Serves 6
1 4- to 5-pound leg of lamb
1/4 cup finely chopped parsley
2 cloves garlic, minced
1/2 teaspoon dried marjoram
2 sprigs rosemary, chopped, or
1/2 teaspoon dried rosemary
1/4 pound Parma ham, cut into 1/2-inch-wide strips
salt and freshly ground pepper to taste
1/4 cup olive oil
1-1/2 cups dry white wine
3 or 4 carrots, halved
6 to 8 new potatoes
6 to 8 small boiling onions

Wipe meat with a damp cloth and make several slashes over the surface. Mix together parsley, garlic, marjoram and rosemary and brush mixture over ham strips. Force ham strips into slashes in lamb leg. Rub the lamb with salt and pepper and any remaining herb mixture. Brown the lamb in a Dutch oven in oil. When meat is browned, add wine and vegetables. Cover and simmer for 40 minutes or until tender, basting occasionally with pan juices and adding a little water if needed.

ZUCCHINI STUFFED WITH LAMB AND PINE NUTS

Serves 6 to 8
8 medium-sized zucchini
1 tablespoon olive oil
1/2 cup pine nuts
4 tablespoons butter
1 pound ground lamb or veal
1 medium-sized onion, chopped
pinch of dried rosemary
1 teaspoon salt
1/8 teaspoon freshly ground pepper
accompaniment: 2 cups plain yogurt

Wash and core zucchini, leaving whole. Rub with olive oil. In a large skillet sauté pine nuts in 2 tablespoons of the butter until golden; remove from pan and set aside. In the same skillet, add remaining butter and brown meat and onion. Combine meat, nuts, and seasonings. Cool mixture and stuff cored zucchini with meat mixture. Place stuffed zucchini in pan; add 1/2 cup water, cover and simmer for 20 minutes, or until zucchini are tender. Serve with yogurt.

STUFFED ZUCCHINI
WITH LAMB AND BULGUR

Serves 6

12 medium-sized zucchini
1 pound ground lamb
1 cup bulgur, soaked in water to cover
   15 minutes and drained
1 teaspoon salt
1/2 teaspoon ground allspice
1 6-ounce can tomato paste
2 tablespoons olive oil
2 cloves garlic, minced
2 tablespoons fresh lemon juice

Cut zucchini in half lengthwise and scoop out centers. Dice pulp and add lamb, bulgur, salt and allspice. Mix well and fill zucchini halves with this stuffing. Place zucchini in one layer in a buttered baking dish. Combine tomato paste, olive oil, garlic and lemon juice and spread over zucchini. Add 2 cups water to pan. Cover with aluminum foil and bake in a preheated 350° oven for 45 minutes.

LAMB

LAMB RISOTTO

Serves 6
4 tablespoons butter
1 medium-sized onion, sliced
1-1/2 pounds boneless lamb, cut into 1-inch cubes
2 cups peeled, seeded and chopped ripe tomatoes
salt and freshly ground pepper to taste
pinch of ground cinnamon
2-1/2 cups long-grain rice
3 cups each lamb or chicken stock and water, heated
3/4 cup grated Parmesan cheese

Melt butter in a flameproof casserole and sauté onion until brown. Add meat and brown on all sides. Add tomatoes, salt, pepper and cinnamon. Cover and simmer 1 hour. Raise heat and add rice with 1 cup of the stock. Cook uncovered for 5 minutes or until the rice has absorbed the stock. Add remaining stock, cup by cup, until all the stock has been absorbed. Sprinkle with Parmesan and serve immediately.

MIXED MEATLOAF WITH APPLES AND PRUNES

Serves 8 to 10
1 pound ground lamb
1 pound ground pork
1 pound ground veal
1 onion, chopped
1 tablespoon salt
1/2 teaspoon freshly ground pepper
1/2 teaspoon ground allspice
1/2 cup bread crumbs
1/2 cup milk
1 cup dried sliced apples, plumped in 1 cup warm water
1 cup dried pitted prunes, plumped in 1 cup warm water

Combine meats, onion, seasonings, bread crumbs and milk. Place half of the meat mixture in a buttered, 3-quart casserole. Drain dried fruits, reserving soaking water, and place fruit on top of meat mixture. Top with remaining meat mixture. Pack firmly. Pour soaking water over all. Cover and bake in a preheated 350° oven for 1-1/2 hours.

MOUSSAKA

Serves 6

2 eggplants, peeled, sliced 1/2 inch thick, salted,
    drained and dried on paper toweling
flour
corn oil as needed
1 onion, minced
1 pound ground lamb
5 tablespoons butter
2 tablespoons tomato paste
1/2 cup minced parsley
1/4 cup dry red wine
freshly ground pepper
1/4 teaspoon ground cinnamon
1 egg, beaten
1/4 cup bread crumbs
2 cups White Sauce, page 51
2 egg yolks, slightly beaten
freshly grated nutmeg
1/2 cup grated Parmesan cheese

Sprinkle eggplant slices lightly with flour. In a skillet, fry eggplant until golden in oil. Remove from skillet and set aside. Pour off oil, return skillet to heat and sauté onion and lamb in butter; add tomato paste, parsley, wine, pepper, cinnamon and egg and mix well. Sprinkle half the bread crumbs in a buttered 2-quart baking dish. Top with a layer of eggplant slices and meat mixture; repeat layers until all ingredients have been used, finishing with a layer of eggplant. Make White Sauce, beating in egg yolks and nutmeg at last minute; pour over top of moussaka, sprinkle with remaining bread crumbs and the Parmesan cheese. Bake in a preheated 350° oven for 1 hour or until top is golden.

LAMB

LAMB BAKED WITH
TOMATOES AND POTATOES

Serves 6
1 large onion, sliced
2 tablespoons each olive oil and butter
2 pounds boneless lamb, cut into 1-inch cubes
2 sprigs rosemary, chopped, or
1/2 teaspoon dried rosemary
1/2 cup dry white wine
1 teaspoon salt
1/2 teaspoon freshly ground pepper
2 cups peeled, seeded and chopped ripe tomatoes
1-1/2 pounds new potatoes

Oven Method
In a 2-quart flameproof casserole sauté onion in olive oil and butter until transparent; add lamb and rosemary and brown meat on all sides. Add wine and simmer until wine evaporates. Sprinkle with salt and pepper. Add tomatoes and potatoes and place casserole in a preheated 375° oven. Bake, covered, for 1 hour.

Slow Cooker Method
Sauté onion in olive oil and butter until transparent in a skillet or a slow cooker with a browning unit. Add lamb and rosemary and brown meat on all sides. Cut potatoes into quarters, place in bottom of a slow cooker and top with all remaining ingredients. Cook, covered, on low 6 to 8 hours.

LAMB CURRY

Serves 6
3 cloves garlic
1 tablespoon grated ginger root
2 whole cloves
1 2-inch piece cinnamon stick
3 cardamom pods, peeled
1/4 cup coriander leaves and stems
2 to 4 dried red chili peppers, seeded
1/2 teaspoon salt
2 tablespoons brown sugar
1 cup coconut milk, page 24
2 pounds boneless lamb, cut into 1-inch cubes
3 tablespoons each butter and corn oil
4 large onions, thinly sliced
1 tart apple, peeled and chopped
freshly cooked rice

suggested accompaniments: chutney, raisins, chopped, roasted or fried cashews, grated coconut, sliced bananas, chopped bell pepper, chopped cucumber, chopped green onions, chopped coriander, hard-cooked eggs with whites and yolks chopped separately

Purée garlic, spices, sugar and coconut milk in a blender and marinate lamb in this mixture for 2 or more hours. Heat butter and oil in a large skillet and sauté onions until transparent. Lower heat, add lamb, marinade and apple and simmer for 30 minutes or until lamb is tender. Serve over a bed of hot rice with as many of the condiments as desired.

LAMB

MUSTARD COATED LAMB

Serves 2 or 3
1/4 cup toasted sesame seeds
12 saltines (crackers)
Dijon-style mustard
6 slices cooked lamb, sliced 1/4 inch thick
2 tablespoons each butter and corn oil
6 slices pumpernickel bread
garnish:
    watercress sprigs
    tomato slices

Combine the sesame seeds and saltines in a blender to make fine crumbs, and transfer to a plate. Spread mustard on both sides of the lamb slices and roll slices in crumbs. Sauté in butter and oil in a skillet until lamb is lightly browned on both sides. Place lamb slices on bread. Garnish with watercress and tomato slices.

Variations Cooked turkey, roast beef or roast pork slices may be substituted for the lamb.

LAMB CHOPS WITH ARTICHOKES

Serves 6 to 8
2 pounds lamb chops, cut 3/4 inch thick
1 clove garlic, minced
1 onion, chopped
1/2 teaspoon dried marjoram
3 tablespoons olive oil
salt and freshly ground pepper to taste
1 cup dry white wine
1 tablespoon tomato paste
1 12-ounce package frozen artichoke hearts,
    thawed
accompaniment:
    boiled new potatoes
    1/4 cup chopped parsley

In a large skillet brown lamb with garlic, onion and marjoram in oil. Season with salt and pepper, add wine and cook over medium heat until wine evaporates. Mix tomato paste with 1 cup water and add to pan. Add artichokes, cover and simmer for 30 minutes. Remove to a warm platter and serve, surrounded by new potatoes sprinkled with chopped parsley.

SAFFRON RICE WITH SPICY LAMB

Serves 8
2 cups long-grain rice, washed and drained
1/4 teaspoon saffron threads, dissolved in
1/4 cup hot water
2 onions, sliced
1/4 pound butter (or half butter and half
    corn oil)
1/4 cup unsalted cashews
1/4 cup slivered blanched almonds
1/3 cup raisins
1 tablespoon minced ginger root
2 cloves garlic, minced
1/2 teaspoon ground cumin
2 pounds boneless lamb, cut into 1-inch cubes
1 stick cinnamon
1/4 teaspoon powdered cloves
1/4 teaspoon cayenne pepper
1/4 teaspoon ground cardamom
1/4 teaspoon freshly grated nutmeg
1-1/2 cups chicken stock
1 cup plain yogurt
salt and freshly ground pepper to taste

In a flameproof casserole or in a large saucepan, bring 2 quarts water to boil. Add rice, lower heat and simmer covered for 10 minutes; drain and set aside, covering with saffron water. Sauté onions in half of the butter until golden. With a slotted spoon remove onions to a plate. Sauté nuts in same pan, adding more butter if needed. With a slotted spoon remove nuts to a plate and set aside. Repeat procedure with raisins. Add remaining butter to pan and cook ginger root, garlic and cumin 1 minute. Add meat, browning on all sides. Blend in remaining spices, 3/4 cup of the stock and yogurt. Cover and simmer 20 minutes. Spoon reserved rice evenly over lamb mixture and sprinkle remaining stock over rice. Cover again and simmer for 15 minutes. Serve lamb and rice on a large platter, with cinnamon stick removed, and reserved onions, nuts and raisins sprinkled on top.

PORK

PORK WITH ZUCCHINI AND CORN, MEXICAN STYLE

Serves 6

2 cloves garlic, minced
1 onion, chopped
2 tablespoons olive oil
1-1/2 pounds boneless pork butt,
    cut into 1-inch cubes
2 cups tomatillo pulp*
1/2 teaspoon dried oregano
2 fresh green chili peppers, seeded and chopped
salt and freshly ground pepper to taste
1 pound zucchini, cut into small chunks
2 cups freshly grated corn kernels
1/2 teaspoon sugar
1 cup pitted black olives

garnish: coriander sprigs
accompaniments:
    sour cream
    warm tortillas or French bread

Sauté the garlic and onion in oil in a skillet or flameproof casserole. Add the pork, tomatillo pulp, oregano, chilies and 1 cup of water. Season with salt and pepper and bring just to a boil. Lower heat, cover and simmer for 45 minutes. Add zucchini, corn, sugar and olives and cook for 10 minutes or until vegetables are tender. Garnish with coriander sprigs, top with dollops of sour cream and serve with tortillas or bread.

*A variety of green tomato available fresh in Mexican markets; also available in cans.

PORK

BIGOS

Serves 6
1 onion, chopped
1 clove garlic, minced
2 tablespoons butter or lard
1 pound cabbage, shredded
1 quart sauerkraut, rinsed and drained
1/4 pound mushrooms, sliced
1 pound boneless pork butt, cut into 1-inch cubes
1 pound boneless veal, cut into 1-inch cubes
1/2 pound Polish sausage, sliced 1/2 inch thick
1 cup beef stock
1 cup peeled and chopped ripe tomatoes
2 tart apples, peeled and diced
1/2 cup pitted prunes
1 bay leaf
1 teaspoon salt
1/2 teaspoon freshly ground pepper
1 cup red wine

Top-of-the-Stove Method
In a Dutch oven sauté onion and garlic in butter until onion is transparent. Add remaining ingredients, cover and simmer for 2 hours.

Slow Cooker Method
Combine all the ingredients, reducing stock and wine to 1/2 cup each, and cook on low, covered, 8 to 10 hours.

Pressure Cooker Method
In a pressure cooker sauté the onion and garlic in butter until onion is transparent. Combine the remaining ingredients, adding 1-1/2 cups water, and cover and bring to full pressure. When steam appears, reduce heat and cook on low 30 minutes. Reduce pressure completely and let stand 10 to 15 minutes to blend flavors.

Wet Clay Cooker Method
Combine all ingredients in a pre-soaked unglazed clay cooker, cover and place in a cold oven. Turn oven to 400° and bake 1-1/2 hours. Remove from oven and let rest 15 minutes before serving.

SZEKELY GULYAS
(Pork and Sauerkraut Stew)

Serves 6
2 onions, chopped
2 tablespoons lard
2 cloves garlic, minced
1 teaspoon caraway seeds
2 tablespoons paprika
2 pounds boneless pork butt, cut into 1-inch cubes
1 teaspoon salt
3 cups sauerkraut, rinsed and drained
1 tablespoon flour
2 cups (1 pint) sour cream
accompaniment: buttered noodles

Top-of-the-Stove Method
(Dutch oven, large skillet or saucepan may be used)
Sauté onions in lard until they become transparent; then add garlic, caraway seeds, paprika and 1 cup water. Bring to a boil and add meat and salt. Lower heat, cover and simmer for 1 hour. Add sauerkraut and continue cooking for 25 minutes. Mix the flour with the sour cream and add to the stew, simmering for 5 minutes. Serve with buttered noodles.

Slow Cooker Method
Combine all ingredients, except flour and sour cream, adding 1/2 cup water. Cook on low, covered, for 8 to 10 hours. Uncover and turn on high. Mix the flour with the sour cream, add to the stew and continue cooking for 5 to 10 minutes to heat through. Serve with buttered noodles.

Pressure Cooker Method
In a pressure cooker sauté onions in lard until they become transparent. Then add remaining ingredients except sauerkraut, flour and sour cream. Add 1-1/2 cups water. Cover and bring to full pressure. When steam appears, reduce heat and cook on low 20 minutes. Reduce pressure completely, uncover and add sauerkraut. Cover and cook for 25 minutes, not under pressure. Mix the flour with the sour cream and add to the stew, simmering for 5 minutes. Serve with buttered noodles.

PORK

PORK MEATBALLS WITH POTATOES

Serves 3 or 4

1 pound lean ground pork
1/8 teaspoon freshly grated nutmeg
1/2 teaspoon salt
1/2 teaspoon freshly ground pepper
1-1/2 cups fresh bread crumbs
1 egg, beaten
1/4 cup corn oil
3 tablespoons butter
2 tablespoons minced shallots
1 clove garlic, minced
2 onions, sliced
4 potatoes, peeled and quartered
1/2 cup dry white wine
1 cup chicken stock
garnish: chopped parsley

Combine the pork, nutmeg, salt, pepper, bread crumbs and egg. Form into meatballs, each about the size of a large egg. Heat the oil in a skillet and brown the meatballs on all sides. Remove to a plate. Pour off excess oil remaining in skillet, add butter and sauté shallots, garlic and onions for 2 minutes. Return meatballs to skillet, surround with potatoes and pour wine and stock over all. Bring to a boil, lower heat, cover and simmer for 25 minutes or until the potatoes are tender. Sprinkle with parsley and serve.

PORK AND VEGETABLE STIR-FRY

Following directions for Beef and Vegetable Stir-Fry, page 114, substitute 1 pound lean pork butt, cut into thin strips, for the beef and use only 1 tablespoon soy sauce or oyster sauce. When stir-frying pork, cook thoroughly, about 3 minutes, before removing to plate.

POZOLE

Serves 6 to 8
1 pound pork butt, cut into 1-1/2-inch pieces
1 3-pound chicken, disjointed
3 pig's feet, split
2 pork tongues
2 onions, chopped
4 to 6 cloves garlic
1 teaspoon salt
6 peppercorns
2 bay leaves
2 or more tablespoons chili powder
1 teaspoon dried oregano
1 pound nixtamal hominy*, well rinsed, or
1 # 2-1/2 can hominy, drained**
accompaniments:
   chopped fresh coriander, lime wedges,
     sliced radishes, chopped red onions,
      shredded lettuce and Tomato Salsa, page 129
   warm tortillas or crusty bread

*Fermented corn available in Mexican markets.
**If using canned hominy, add the last 10 minutes of
cooking time.

Top-of-the-Stove Method
Combine pork butt, chicken, pig's feet, tongues, onions, garlic, salt, peppercorns and bay leaves with 3 quarts water in a soup pot. Bring to a boil, lower heat and simmer, covered, 1 hour. Add chili powder, oregano and nixtamal hominy and continue cooking until meats are tender, about 1 to 1-1/2 hours. Lift tongue from pot, remove and discard skin and cut meat into pieces; return meat to stew. Serve in soup plates with accompaniments.

Pressure Cooker Method
Combine all the ingredients with water to cover, cover and bring to full pressure. When steam appears, reduce heat and cook on low 30 minutes. Reduce pressure completely and let stand 15 minutes to blend flavors. If canned hominy is used, add it at the end of the cooking period and cook 10 minutes, not under pressure. Lift tongue from pot, remove and discard skin and cut meat into pieces. Return meat to stew. Serve in soup plates with accompaniments.

PORK

PORK, SAUERKRAUT
AND BARLEY CASSEROLE

Serves 6
1 3-pound pork loin roast or pork butt
1-1/2 quarts sauerkraut, rinsed and drained
1 onion, thinly sliced
1/2 cup pearl barley, rinsed and drained
2 bay leaves
1/2 teaspoon freshly ground pepper

Oven Method
Place pork in Dutch oven or large casserole. Top with sauerkraut and onion. Sprinkle barley over sauerkraut. Tuck in bay leaves and grind pepper over top. Pour water to the top of the sauerkraut (about 1 quart) and cover. Bake in a preheated 350° oven for 3 hours. Remove pork, slice and serve with sauerkraut-barley mixture.

Slow Cooker Method
Place ingredients in slow cooker as directed in oven method, reducing water to 2 cups. Cook on low, covered, 10 to 12 hours. Serve as directed in oven method.

ROAST LOIN OF PORK
WITH POTATOES AND APPLES

Serves 6
1 5- to 6-pound loin of pork with some fat on it
salt and freshly ground pepper to taste
pinch of ground allspice
6 medium-sized onions
6 medium-sized potatoes, peeled
6 baking apples, cored
1 to 2 teaspoons cornstarch
1 cup apple cider
1/2 cup applejack or Calvados

Rub the loin of pork with salt, pepper and allspice and place in a roasting pan. Surround with onions and potatoes and roast, covered, in a preheated 325° oven for 1-1/2 to 2 hours. Uncover, add apples and continue roasting 1 hour longer to brown meat. Allow 35 minutes per pound of meat; meat thermometer will read 170° when roast is done. Turn potatoes and onions during cooking. Remove meat to a warm platter and surround with potatoes, onions and apples. Pour off excess fat from the pan. Mix cornstarch with the apple cider and applejack. Add to the pan and stir over high heat on stovetop, until sauce begins to thicken. Simmer 5 minutes. Slice roast and pour sauce over slices to serve.

CALIFORNIA HASH

Serves 4 to 6
3/4 pound lean ground pork
3/4 pound lean ground beef
1 teaspoon salt
1/2 teaspoon freshly ground pepper
1/2 cup dry sherry
1 onion, chopped
2 cloves garlic, minced
1 bell pepper, chopped
3 tablespoons capers
1/2 cup pitted green olives, sliced
3 tablespoons olive oil
1 bay leaf
1/4 teaspoon ground cumin
1/2 teaspoon dried oregano
3/4 cup tomato sauce
1/2 cup raisins
1/2 cup slivered blanched almonds
accompaniment: tortillas or French bread

Combine the meats, salt, pepper and sherry and let stand for 1 hour. In a skillet sauté the onion, garlic, bell pepper, capers and olives in the oil. Blend in the meat mixture, bay leaf, cumin, oregano, tomato sauce, raisins and almonds. Cover and cook over low heat for 40 minutes. Serve with warm tortillas or French bread.

PORK

HUNGARIAN CABBAGE ROLLS

Serves 6 to 8
1 large head cabbage
3/4 pound ground pork
3/4 pound ground beef
1 small onion, chopped
1 cup rice
1 egg, beaten
1 tablespoon salt
1/2 teaspoon freshly ground pepper
1 tablespoon paprika
2 cups sauerkraut, rinsed and drained
2 cups each tomato juice and water
1 cup (1/2 pint) sour cream

Top-of-the-Stove Method
(Dutch oven, large soup pot or large skillet may be used)

Remove core from cabbage, place in a large bowl and pour boiling water over to cover. Let stand until the cabbage has wilted, about 5 minutes. Drain and remove the leaves, leaving them whole. Trim off the heavy stem and flatten the leaves. Combine the meats, onion, rice, egg, salt, pepper and paprika. Put about 2 tablespoons of this mixture on each cabbage leaf, fold sides in like an envelope and roll up. Place rolls seam side down in pot. Spread the sauerkraut on top of the rolls and add tomato juice and water. Bring to a boil, reduce heat, cover and simmer for 1-1/2 hours. Carefully lift the cabbage rolls out onto a warm platter. Blend 1/2 cup of the broth from the pot with the sour cream and pour over the cabbage rolls.

Slow Cooker Method
Proceed with recipe as for top-of-the-stove method, reducing tomato juice and water to 1-1/2 cups each. Cook on low, covered, for 6 to 8 hours. Remove cabbage rolls and complete recipe as directed for top-of-the-stove method.

Pressure Cooker Method
Proceed with recipe as for top-of-the-stove method. Cover and bring to full pressure. When steam appears, reduce heat and cook on low for 20 minutes. Reduce pressure completely and let stand covered 10 to 15 minutes to blend flavors. Lift out cabbage rolls and complete recipe as directed for top-of-the-stove method.

STUFFED WHOLE CABBAGE

Serves 6 to 8
1 large curly Savoy cabbage
1/2 pound bulk pork sausage
1-1/2 pounds ground veal
1 cup chopped mushrooms
1 onion, chopped
2 cloves garlic, minced
1 teaspoon salt
1/2 teaspoon freshly ground pepper
2 tablespoons butter or olive oil
2 onions, quartered
4 carrots, sliced
2 turnips, sliced
2 cups beef stock or water
1 bay leaf
1/2 teaspoon dried thyme
1 cup fresh peas (1 pound, unshelled)
accompaniment: French bread

Top-of-the-Stove Method
Place cabbage in a large bowl and pour boiling water over to cover. Let stand 5 minutes or until limp. Combine meats, mushrooms, chopped onion, garlic, salt and pepper and stuff mixture between all leaves except the two outer leaves. Tie cabbage firmly with string, pressing back into original shape. Place cabbage in a large soup pot. Surround with remaining ingredients, except peas. Cover, bring to a boil, reduce heat and simmer for 1-1/2 hours or until cabbage is cooked through. Add peas for last 5 minutes of cooking time. To serve, cut cabbage into wedges and serve with vegetables. Strain broth and serve in cups, accompanied with French bread.

Slow Cooker Method
Prepare cabbage as directed for top-of-the-stove method and place in slow cooker with all remaining ingredients, except peas. Cook on low, covered, for 6 to 8 hours. Add peas, cover and cook on high for 15 minutes.

Pressure Cooker Method
Prepare cabbage as directed for top-of-the-stove method. Place in pressure cooker with all remaining ingredients, except peas, increasing stock to 3 cups and cutting vegetables into chunks rather than slices. Cover and bring to full pressure. When steam appears, reduce heat and cook on low for 20 minutes. Reduce pressure completely, uncover and add peas. Cover and continue cooking for 5 minutes, not under pressure. Let stand, covered, for 10 to 15 minutes to blend flavors.

PORK

RICE WITH ITALIAN SAUSAGE AND ZUCCHINI

Serves 4
1/2 pound Italian sausages, sliced 1/2 inch thick
1 onion, chopped
2 tablespoons each butter and olive oil
1 pound zucchini, sliced 1/4 inch thick
1/2 cup dry white wine
3 to 4 cups chicken stock
1 cup rice
3 sprigs parsley, finely chopped
3/4 cup grated Parmesan cheese

In a skillet sauté sausages and onion in butter and oil until sausage is browned. Add zucchini slices and sauté for 2 minutes. Pour in wine and cook until evaporated. Add stock and bring to a boil. Add rice, reduce heat to low and cook until rice is tender, about 20 minutes. When rice has thoroughly absorbed stock, stir in parsley and Parmesan and serve immediately.

STUFFED LETTUCE, PARISIAN STYLE

Serves 4
8 large romaine or iceberg lettuce leaves
1 pound bulk pork sausage
1 teaspoon dried marjoram
2 tablespoons chopped chives
2 tablespoons chopped parsley
1 small bell pepper, chopped
3/4 cup fresh bread crumbs
1 egg, beaten
1/2 cup milk
3/4 cup tomato sauce
3 tablespoons butter
accompaniment: French bread

Pour boiling water over the lettuce leaves and let stand for 2 minutes, or until just limp. Drain and pat leaves dry. Combine the remaining ingredients except the tomato sauce and butter. Divide filling mixture into 8 portions and place each on a lettuce leaf. Fold sides in like an envelope and roll up. Place seam side down in a buttered baking dish. Pour tomato sauce over the stuffed leaves. Dot with butter. Cover with foil and bake in a preheated 350° oven for 40 minutes. Remove foil and bake 10 minutes longer to brown top lightly. Serve with French bread.

Variations Substitute any minced raw or cooked meat, fish or poultry for the pork sausage.

STUFFED EGGPLANT, CREOLE STYLE

Serves 4

2 eggplants, about 1 pound each
1/4 cup olive oil
3 tablespoons butter
1 small onion, chopped
2 green onions, chopped
2 cloves garlic, minced
1 cup peeled and chopped ripe tomatoes
1/2 teaspoon dried thyme
1/4 teaspoon cayenne pepper
1/2 teaspoon freshly ground pepper
1/2 pound ground cooked ham
2 cups fresh French bread crumbs
2 tablespoons chopped coriander or parsley

Cut the eggplants in half lengthwise and remove pulp to make a scooped-out shell, 1/2 inch thick. Chop the eggplant pulp and set aside. Heat the olive oil in a large skillet and gently cook the eggplant shells, cut side down, for 5 minutes. Turn shells over, cover and cook 5 minutes longer. Remove shells to a shallow baking dish. Add butter to pan, with any remaining oil, and sauté onions and garlic for 2 minutes. Add reserved eggplant pulp, tomatoes, thyme, cayenne and pepper and cook over brisk heat until most of the liquid has evaporated and the mixture is thick. Remove from heat and mix in ham, bread crumbs and coriander. Fill the eggplant shells and bake in a preheated 400° oven for 15 minutes or until slightly browned.

SCALLOPED POTATOES AND HAM

Serves 4

2 cups diced cooked ham
2 pounds potatoes, peeled and thinly sliced
2 cups milk
1/2 teaspoon dry mustard
1 small onion, grated
3 tablespoons butter

Butter the bottom and sides of a 2-quart baking dish. Beginning with the ham, alternate layers of ham and potatoes, finishing with a layer of potatoes. Combine the milk, mustard and onion, and pour over all. Dot with butter. Cover and bake in a preheated 325° oven for 1 hour or until potatoes are tender. Remove cover and continue cooking for 15 minutes or until browned.

PORK

BRAISED HAM
WITH MADEIRA AND RAISIN SAUCE
(Served with Baked Yams)

Serves 10 or more
3/4 cup raisins
1-1/2 cups Madeira
1 10-pound precooked smoked ham
1 cup beef stock
1 onion, stuck with 2 cloves
1 bay leaf
1 teaspoon cornstarch, dissolved in
1 tablespoon water
5 orange slices, halved
1 tablespoon butter
garnish: watercress sprigs

Soak raisins in Madeira overnight. Remove skin from ham, leaving a 1/4-inch layer of fat. Put the ham in a roasting pan. Drain raisins, reserving Madeira, and set aside. Add the Madeira, stock, onion and bay leaf to the pan. Braise the ham in a preheated 350° oven for 1-1/2 hours. Baste every 20 minutes during cooking. Transfer the ham to a warm platter, remove onion and bay leaf from the pan and skim off as much fat as possible. Place the pan over high heat on stovetop and reduce juices to 1-1/2 cups. Thicken with cornstarch mixture. Add the reserved raisins and orange slices and simmer for 5 minutes. Stir in the butter until melted. Slice ham and garnish with the orange slices and watercress. Pour 1/2 cup sauce over the ham and serve remaining sauce on the side.

Baked Yams
Scrub yams, 1 per serving, and place on oven rack in a preheated 350° oven (these can bake on the rack above the ham) for 1 hour or more, depending on the size of the yams, until tender. Serve with butter and a pinch of freshly grated nutmeg.

SCHNITZ UND KNEPPE

Serves 6 to 8
1 3-pound smoked ham with bone
2 cups dried apples
1 tablespoon brown sugar

Dumplings
1-1/2 cups unbleached white flour
1 tablespoon baking powder
1/2 teaspoon salt
2 tablespoons butter
1/4 cup milk
1 egg, well beaten

In a large saucepan or Dutch oven place ham with cold water to cover and bring to a rapid boil. Skim any surface scum. Lower heat, cover and simmer for 1 hour. While ham is cooking, soak apples in water for 1 hour and drain. Add apples and brown sugar to pot and continue simmering for 1 hour. Remove ham to platter and surround with apples; keep warm. Reserve ham broth to make dumplings.

To make dumplings, sift together the flour, baking powder and salt. Cut butter into flour mixture with 2 knives or a pastry blender. Combine the milk and egg and add to the flour and butter mixture, mixing well. Bring ham broth to a boil and drop in dumplings from a soup spoon. Cover tightly and simmer 10 to 12 minutes. Lift dumplings out with a slotted spoon and arrange on the platter with the ham and apples. Spoon a little ham broth over all.

MEAT-AND-SPINACH ROLLS

Serves 4
1-1/2 cups chopped cooked spinach
2 hard-cooked eggs, chopped
2 tablespoons butter, melted
salt and freshly ground pepper to taste
pinch of freshly grated nutmeg
12 thin slices cooked meat, such as ham,
    beef, lamb or tongue
8 ounces wide egg noodles, cooked al dente and
    tossed lightly with butter
1 tablespoon prepared horseradish
1 teaspoon Dijon-style mustard
3/4 cup heavy cream

Combine spinach, eggs, butter, salt, pepper and nutmeg. Place a spoonful of the mixture on each slice of meat and roll up, fastening with toothpicks. Layer bottom of buttered casserole with cooked noodles. Place rolls on top. Combine remaining ingredients and pour over all. Bake in a preheated 400° oven for 20 minutes or until heated through.

BEEF

OVEN POT ROAST WITH ONION GRAVY

Serves 6 to 8
1 4-pound beef pot roast (rump, round or chuck)
1/2 teaspoon ground cinnamon
1/2 teaspoon freshly grated nutmeg
1 teaspoon dry mustard
1 teaspoon salt
1/2 teaspoon freshly ground pepper
4 large onions, sliced
2 cups beef stock
accompaniments:
    freshly cooked noodles
    sliced tomatoes and cucumbers

Rub the meat with a mixture of the cinnamon, nutmeg, mustard, salt and pepper. Place meat in a roasting pan, surround with onions and pour in stock. Cover and bake in a preheated 300° oven for 3 hours. Slice and serve with freshly cooked noodles and sliced tomatoes and cucumbers.

Variations
• Add 1 cup mushrooms to the roast for the last hour of cooking.
• Add 2 cups fresh peas for the last 30 minutes of cooking.
• Blend 1 cup (1/2 pint) sour cream into the pan juices and heat through before serving.

BEEF

BEEF BOURGUIGNON

Serves 6

1/4 pound salt pork, well rinsed and cut into
   1/2-inch dice
2 pounds lean boneless beef, cut into 1-inch cubes
1 cup beef stock
1 cup Burgundy
2 sprigs parsley
1/4 teaspoon dried thyme
1 bay leaf
1 carrot, grated
1/2 teaspoon freshly ground pepper
2 tablespoons butter
6 to 8 small boiling onions
1/2 pound small button mushrooms
1 cup fresh peas (1 pound, unshelled)
garnish: chopped parsley
accompaniment: freshly cooked rice

Top-of-the-Stove Method
Sauté salt pork in a Dutch oven until fat is rendered; do not brown. Remove salt pork with a slotted spoon and add beef, browning on all sides. Add reserved salt pork, stock, Burgundy, parsley, thyme, bay leaf, carrot and pepper. Bring just to a boil, cover, lower heat and simmer for 1 to 1-1/2 hours or until meat is tender. Add butter, onions and mushrooms and continue cooking, covered, for 15 minutes. Add peas and cook 5 minutes. Serve, garnished with parsley, over rice.

Slow Cooker Method
Sauté salt pork in a skillet or a slow cooker with a browning unit until fat is rendered; do not brown. Remove salt pork with a slotted spoon and add beef, browning on all sides. Combine browned meat, reserved salt pork, only 3/4 cup each beef stock and Burgundy, parsley, thyme, bay leaf, carrot, pepper and onions in a slow cooker. Cover and cook on low 6 to 8 hours. Add butter, mushrooms and peas and cook on high 15 minutes. Serve, garnished with parsley, over rice.

BEEF WITH ONIONS

Serves 2
2 onions, thinly sliced
2 tablespoons butter
1/2 cup tomato sauce
1/2 cup beef stock
1/2 cup dry white wine
4 slices boiled beef (use any leftover boiled beef)
salt and freshly ground pepper to taste
2 tablespoons bread crumbs
accompaniments:
    French bread
    tossed green salad

In a skillet sauté the onions in butter until golden brown, about 5 minutes. Add the tomato sauce, stock and wine and lay the beef slices on top. Simmer for 15 minutes. Salt and pepper lightly. Spoon sauce in skillet over meat with some of the onions. Sprinkle with bread crumbs and place in a preheated 375° oven for 10 minutes or until top is crusty. Serve with French bread and green salad.

Pressure Cooker Method

In a pressure cooker sauté salt pork until fat is rendered; do not brown. Remove salt pork with a slotted spoon and add beef, browning on all sides. Add reserved salt pork, stock, Burgundy, parsley, thyme, bay leaf, carrot, pepper and 1 cup of water. Cover and bring to full pressure. When steam appears, reduce heat and cook on low 20 minutes. Reduce pressure completely, uncover and add butter, onions and mushrooms and continue cooking, covered, 10 minutes, not under pressure. Add peas and cook 5 minutes. Serve, garnished with parsley, over rice.

Wet Clay Cooker Method

Combine all ingredients, except butter, onions, mushrooms and peas, in a pre-soaked unglazed clay cooker, reducing beef stock and Burgundy to 3/4 cup each. Cover and place in a cold oven. Turn oven to 400° and bake 1 hour and 15 minutes. Add butter, onions and mushrooms, cover and bake 15 minutes. Remove from oven, add peas, cover and let stand 10 minutes. Serve, garnished with parsley, over rice.

BEEF

POT ROAST, VIENNESE STYLE

Serves 6 to 8
1 3-1/2- to 4-pound rump roast or sirloin tip
2 tablespoons butter
1 teaspoon salt
1/2 teaspoon freshly ground pepper
1 onion, chopped
2 carrots, chopped
2 turnips, chopped
4 dried figs, chopped
1 cup white wine
1 cup beef stock
8 new potatoes
4 gingersnaps, crushed

Top-of-the-Stove Method
(Dutch oven or flameproof casserole may be used)
Brown the meat on all sides in butter. Add salt, pepper, onion, carrots, turnips and figs. Pour in the wine and stock. Cover and simmer for 1-1/2 hours or until meat is tender. Add potatoes and simmer 20 minutes or until tender. Stir in the gingersnaps to thicken juices.

Slow Cooker Method
Brown meat on all sides in butter in a skillet or a slow cooker with a browning unit. Put carrots, turnips and potatoes in bottom of slow cooker and place roast on top. Add remaining ingredients, except gingersnaps, reducing wine and stock to 3/4 cup each. Cover and cook on low 8 to 10 hours. Add gingersnaps and cook on high, uncovered, until thickened.

Pressure Cooker Method
In a pressure cooker brown meat on all sides in butter. Add salt, pepper, onion, wine, stock and 1 cup water. Cover and bring to full pressure. When steam appears, reduce heat and cook on low 25 minutes. Reduce pressure completely, add remaining vegetables and figs, cover and simmer 20 minutes or until tender, not under pressure. Add gingersnaps and cook, uncovered, until thickened.

Wet Clay Cooker Method
Combine all ingredients, reducing wine and stock to 3/4 cup each, in a pre-soaked unglazed clay cooker. Cover and place in a cold oven. Turn oven to 400° and bake 1-1/2 hours or until meat is tender. Remove from oven and let stand 10 minutes.

POT ROAST, CREOLE STYLE

Serves 6 to 8
2 slices bacon, diced
1 teaspoon freshly ground pepper
1 3-1/2- to 4-pound rump roast or sirloin tip
1 or more fresh green chili peppers, seeded and
   minced
1 bay leaf
1/2 teaspoon dried thyme
2 cups peeled and diced ripe tomatoes
1/2 teaspoon sugar
1 celery rib, chopped
1 onion, chopped
2 cloves garlic, minced
2 tablespoons chopped parsley or coriander
accompaniment: freshly cooked rice or French
   bread

Top-of-the-Stove Method
(Dutch oven or flameproof casserole may be used)
Cook the bacon long enough to release the fat; do
not brown. Remove bacon pieces with a slotted
spoon and set aside. Pepper the meat and brown on
all sides in drippings. Add the remaining ingredients. Cover and simmer for 2 hours or until tender.
Fifteen minutes before the roast is done, add the
bacon pieces to the pan. Slice the meat and serve
with pan juices and rice or French bread.

Slow Cooker Method
Cook the bacon long enough to release the fat in a
skillet or a slow cooker with a browning unit.
Remove bacon with a slotted spoon; set aside.
Pepper the meat and brown on all sides in drip-
pings. Add the remaining ingredients, cover and
cook on low 8 to 10 hours. Add reserved bacon
pieces, cover, turn on high and cook 15 minutes.
Slice the meat and serve with pan juices and rice or
French bread.

Pressure Cooker Method
In a pressure cooker cook the bacon long enough
to release the fat; remove bacon pieces with a
slotted spoon and set aside. Pepper the meat and
brown on all sides in drippings. Add the remaining
ingredients with 1 cup water. Cover and bring to
full pressure. When steam appears, reduce heat and
cook on low 30 minutes. Reduce pressure completely and let stand covered 10 to 15 minutes to
blend flavors. Stir in bacon pieces. Slice meat and
serve with pan juices and rice or French bread.

Wet Clay Cooker Method
Pepper the meat and place in a pre-soaked unglazed
clay cooker. Add remaining ingredients, cover and
place in a cold oven. Turn oven to 400° and bake
for 1-1/2 hours. Remove from oven and let stand
10 minutes. Slice the meat and serve with pan
juices and rice or French bread.

BEEF

CALIFORNIA POT ROAST

Serves 8 to 10
1 4- to 5-pound pot roast
2 teaspoons salt
1/4 teaspoon freshly ground pepper
1/4 teaspoon ground ginger
2 tablespoons each butter and corn oil
2 cloves garlic, minced
3 onions, chopped
1 cup dry red wine
1 cup beef stock
1 cup pitted prunes, soaked in 1 cup water
1/2 pound zucchini, cut into chunks
1 cup small button mushrooms
1 cup pitted ripe olives
accompaniment: French bread

Top-of-the-Stove Method
Rub the roast with the salt, pepper and ginger and brown on all sides in a Dutch oven in butter and oil. Add garlic, onions, wine and stock. Cover and cook over low heat for 1 hour, turning meat occasionally. Add prunes and their liquid. Cover and continue cooking for 45 minutes or until roast is tender. Add zucchini, mushrooms and olives and simmer 15 minutes. Serve with French bread.

Slow Cooker Method
Rub the roast with the salt, pepper and ginger and brown on all sides in butter and oil in a skillet or a slow cooker with a browning unit. Combine meat with remaining ingredients, except zucchini, mushrooms and olives, reducing stock to 1/2 cup and place in a slow cooker; cover and cook on low 8 to 10 hours. Add zucchini, mushrooms and olives, cover and cook on high 20 minutes. Serve with French bread.

Wet Clay Cooker Method
Combine all ingredients except zucchini, mushrooms and olives, reducing wine and stock to 3/4 cup each, in a pre-soaked unglazed clay cooker. Cover and place in a cold oven. Turn oven to 400° and bake 1-1/2 hours. Add zucchini, mushrooms and olives, cover and bake 15 minutes. Remove from oven and let stand 10 minutes. Serve with French bread.

BOILED BEEF AND SAUSAGE WITH VEGETABLES

Serves 6 to 8

1 5-pound beef brisket or rump roast
1/2 pound lean salt pork, blanched
1 bay leaf
1/2 teaspoon dried thyme
8 peppercorns
2 onions, each stuck with 2 cloves
1 pound garlic sausages
6 carrots
4 celery ribs, halved
6 small turnips
2 rutabagas, quartered
1 head Savoy cabbage, cut in wedges
6 leeks
6 to 8 new potatoes
accompaniments: horseradish, Dijon-style mustard,
   dill pickles

Top-of-the-Stove Method

Place the beef and salt pork in a large soup pot with water to cover. Bring to a boil and skim any surface scum. Add bay leaf, thyme, peppercorns and onions. Lower heat, cover and simmer 1-1/2 hours. Add sausages and remaining vegetables and continue simmering for 30 minutes. Remove and slice the meats and place on a warm platter surrounded with the vegetables. Accompany with horseradish, mustard and dill pickles. Strain the broth and serve in cups.

Slow Cooker Method

Combine all ingredients with water to cover in a slow cooker and cook on low, covered, for 8 to 10 hours. Remove and slice the meats and place on a warm platter surrounded with the vegetables. Accompany with horseradish, mustard and pickles. Strain the broth and serve in cups.

BEEF

SOUTH OF THE BORDER STEW

Serves 8

1-1/2 pounds beef chuck, cut into 1-inch cubes
1-1/2 pounds pork butt, cut into 1-inch cubes
3 tablespoons lard
2 cloves garlic, minced
2 onions, chopped
1 or more fresh green chili peppers, seeded and
    chopped
2 sweet red peppers, chopped
2 bay leaves, crumbled
1 teaspoon dried oregano
1/2 teaspoon ground cumin
2 cups peeled and chopped ripe tomatoes
1/4 cup fresh lemon juice
1 cup raisins
1 cup whole blanched almonds
1 teaspoon salt
1 teaspoon freshly ground pepper
1 cup dry red wine
1 cup beef stock
accompaniment: warm tortillas

Oven Method

Brown the meats in the lard in a large flameproof casserole. Add garlic and onions and cook until onions are limp. Add peppers, bay leaves, oregano, cumin and tomatoes. Bring to a boil and cook 5 minutes. Add lemon juice, raisins, almonds, salt and pepper and mix well with meat mixture. Pour the wine and stock over all and place in a pre-heated 300° oven for 2 hours or until the meat is tender. Serve with tortillas.

Slow Cooker Method

Brown the meats in lard in a skillet or a slow cooker with a browning unit. Add garlic and onions and cook until onions are limp. Combine browned meats and remaining ingredients in a slow cooker, reducing wine and stock to 1/2 cup each. Cover and cook on low 8 to 10 hours. Serve with tortillas.

Pressure Cooker Method

In a pressure cooker brown the meats in lard. Add garlic and onions and cook until onions are limp. Add remaining ingredients, cover and bring to full pressure. When steam appears, reduce heat and cook on low 20 minutes. Reduce pressure completely and let stand 10 to 15 minutes to blend flavors. Serve with tortillas.

BEEF AND VEGETABLES
WITH SOUR CREAM

Serves 4 to 6
1 pound lean ground beef
1 onion, chopped
2 tablespoons butter
2 potatoes, peeled and cut into 1/2-inch cubes
1 turnip, cut into 1/4-inch cubes
3 carrots, cut into 1/4-inch cubes
2 celery ribs, cut into 1/2-inch slices
1/4 teaspoon caraway seeds
1/4 teaspoon paprika
1 teaspoon salt

1/4 teaspoon freshly ground pepper
1 cup (1/2 pint) sour cream
1 tablespoon flour
garnish: 2 tablespoons chopped parsley

In a large skillet sauté beef and onion in butter until browned, about 5 minutes. Add the potatoes, turnip, carrots, celery, caraway seeds, paprika, salt and pepper. Cover and cook over medium heat for 15 minutes or until vegetables are tender. Combine sour cream and flour and add to skillet, stirring constantly. Heat through; do not boil. Serve from skillet immediately, garnished with parsley.

BEEF

COTTAGE STEW

Serves 4

1-1/2 pounds lean beef, cut into 1-inch cubes, dusted with
2 tablespoons flour
2 tablespoons each butter and corn oil
2 celery ribs with leaves, cut in chunks
1 cup beef stock
1/2 teaspoon salt
1/4 teaspoon freshly ground pepper
1/2 teaspoon each dried thyme and marjoram
1 teaspoon prepared mustard
2 tablespoons fresh lemon juice
3 tablespoons chopped parsley
accompaniment: toast, boiled noodles or potatoes

Top-of-the-Stove Method

Brown the meat in a Dutch oven in butter and oil. Add celery, stock, salt, pepper, thyme, marjoram and mustard. Cover and simmer for 1-1/2 hours or until meat is tender. Stir in the lemon juice and parsley and serve with toast, noodles or potatoes.

Slow Cooker Method

Brown the meat in butter and oil in a skillet or a slow cooker with a browning unit. Combine meat and remaining ingredients, except lemon juice and parsley, and place in a slow cooker. Cover and cook on low 6 to 8 hours. Stir in lemon juice and parsley and serve with toast, noodles or potatoes.

Pressure Cooker Method

In a pressure cooker brown the meat in butter and oil. Add remaining ingredients, except lemon juice and parsley, adding 1 cup of water. Cover and bring to full pressure. When steam appears, reduce heat and cook on low 20 minutes. Reduce pressure completely and let stand 10 to 15 minutes to blend flavors. Stir in lemon juice and parsley and serve with toast, noodles or potatoes.

MEXICAN BEEF AND GREEN CHILI STEW

Serves 4 to 6
1-1/2 pounds round steak, cut into 1-inch cubes, dusted with
1 tablespoon flour
1 onion, chopped
2 cloves garlic, minced
2 tablespoons lard
4 or more fresh green chili peppers, seeded and chopped
1/2 teaspoon dried oregano
1 cup tomatillo pulp*
garnish: chopped coriander (optional)
accompaniment: warm corn tortillas

Top-of-the-Stove Method
(Dutch oven or large skillet may be used)
Brown the meat with the onion and garlic in lard. Add the chilies, oregano, tomatillo pulp and 1 cup water. Bring just to a boil, cover and simmer for 45 minutes. Garnish with coriander and serve with tortillas.

Slow Cooker Method
Brown the meat with the onion and garlic in lard in a skillet or slow cooker with a browning unit. Combine the meat and remaining ingredients in a slow cooker with 1/2 cup water. Cover and cook on low 6 to 8 hours. Garnish with coriander and serve with tortillas.

Pressure Cooker Method
In a pressure cooker brown the meat, onion and garlic in lard. Add remaining ingredients with 1-1/2 cups water. Cover and bring to full pressure. When steam appears, reduce heat and cook on low 15 minutes. Reduce pressure completely and let stand covered 10 to 15 minutes to blend flavors. Garnish with coriander and serve with tortillas.

*A variety of green tomato available fresh in Mexican markets; also available in cans.

BEEF

BEEF-AND-KIDNEY STEW

Serves 6
1/4 pound mushrooms, halved
4 tablespoons butter
1 cup chopped onions
2 pounds boneless lean beef, cut into
    1-inch cubes, dusted with
1/4 cup flour
2 pairs lamb kidneys, thinly sliced
2 cups beef stock
2 tablespoons chopped parsley
1 teaspoon dried thyme
1/2 bay leaf
1/4 teaspoon freshly ground pepper
pinch of cayenne pepper
1 teaspoon Worcestershire sauce
4 potatoes, peeled and quartered
garnish: chopped parsley

Top-of-the-Stove Method
In a Dutch oven sauté mushrooms in 2 tablespoons of the butter for 5 minutes; remove and set aside. Add remaining butter and brown onions, beef and kidneys. Add remaining ingredients, except potatoes, and bring to a rapid boil. Reduce heat, cover and simmer 1 hour. Add potatoes, cover and simmer 20 minutes. Add reserved mushrooms, cover and cook 10 minutes. Garnish with parsley.

Slow Cooker Method
Sauté mushrooms in 2 tablespoons of the butter in a skillet or a slow cooker with a browning unit for 5 minutes; remove and set aside. Add remaining butter and brown onions, beef and kidneys. Put potatoes in the bottom of a slow cooker and add meat mixture with remaining ingredients, reducing stock to 1-1/2 cups. Cover and cook on low 6 to 8 hours. Add reserved mushrooms, cover and cook on high 15 minutes. Garnish with parsley.

INDIAN CORN STEW

Pressure Cooker Method

In a pressure cooker sauté the mushrooms in 2 tablespoons of the butter for 5 minutes. Remove and set aside. Add remaining butter and brown onions, beef and kidneys. Add remaining ingredients, except potatoes, with 1 cup water. Cover and bring to full pressure. When steam appears, reduce heat and cook on low 15 minutes. Reduce pressure completely, add potatoes, cover and simmer 20 minutes, not under pressure. Add reserved mushrooms; simmer 10 minutes. Garnish with parsley.

Wet Clay Cooker Method

Combine all ingredients, reducing stock to 1-1/2 cups, in a pre-soaked unglazed clay cooker. Cover and place in a cold oven. Turn oven to 400° and bake 1-1/2 hours. Remove from oven and let stand 10 minutes. Garnish with parsley.

Serves 4

1 pound lean ground beef
1 onion, chopped
1 clove garlic, minced
2 tablespoons lard
1 or more fresh green chili peppers,
    seeded and chopped
1 bell pepper, chopped
3 cups freshly grated corn kernels
3 ripe tomatoes, peeled and coarsely chopped
1 tablespoon sugar
1 teaspoon salt
1/2 teaspoon freshly ground pepper
accompaniment: tortillas or French bread

In a skillet sauté meat, onion and garlic in the lard until meat loses its redness. Add the chilies, bell pepper, corn, tomatoes and seasonings. Cover and simmer for 20 minutes. Serve with warm tortillas or crusty bread.

BEEF

BEEF AND VEGETABLE STIR-FRY

Serves 4

1 pound flank or skirt steak, cut into thin strips
1 small onion, thinly sliced (optional)
1 or 2 slices ginger root, minced (optional)
1 clove garlic, minced
2 tablespoons soy sauce or oyster sauce
1/2 teaspoon sugar
1 tablespoon sherry
4 tablespoons peanut oil
1 pound prepared vegetable or combination
   (see following)
water as needed, depending upon vegetable
binder:
   2 teaspoons cornstarch, dissolved in
   1/4 cup water
accompaniment: freshly cooked rice

Combine meat, onion, ginger root, garlic, soy sauce, sugar and sherry. Heat 2 tablespoons of the oil in a wok or skillet over high heat and stir-fry meat mixture 1 minute or until meat loses its redness. Remove to plate. Return wok to heat and add remaining oil. Stir-fry vegetable 10 seconds and add water, if necessary. Cover and let steam rise to surface, about 1 or 2 minutes. Return meat to wok and bind with cornstarch mixture. Serve immediately with rice.

Variation with Chili When heating oil before stir-frying meat, add 2 small dried red chili peppers and stir-fry until chilies are browned. Discard chilies; proceed with recipe, stir-frying meat in same oil.

Vegetables with High-Moisture Content The following vegetables require little or no water in cooking: bok choy, cut into 2-inch lengths, Napa or head cabbage, coarsely shredded; cucumbers, thinly sliced; bean sprouts; spinach, leaves left whole or halved if large; tomatoes, cut into wedges.

Vegetables with Low-Moisture Content The following vegetables require the addition of about 1/3 cup of water to create steam in cooking: asparagus, sliced diagonally 1/4 inch thick; bamboo shoots, thinly sliced, cut into matchstick or diced; bell pepper, cut into 1-inch chunks, thinly sliced or diced; broccoli, cut into 2-inch flowerets and stems sliced 1/4 inch thick; carrots, thinly sliced, cut into matchstick or diced; cauliflower, cut into 2-inch flowerets and stems sliced 1/4 inch thick; celery, sliced diagonally 1/4 inch thick or cut into 1/2-inch dice; eggplant, cut into 1-inch chunks; kohlrabi, thinly sliced, cut into matchstick or into 1/2-inch dice; peas; snow peas, left whole or halved if large; hard or winter squash, cut into 1/4-inch-thick slices or into 1/2-inch dice; string beans and Chinese long beans, snapped or cut into 2-inch lengths; turnips, cut into 1/4-inch-thick slices or into 1/2-inch dice; water chestnuts, thinly sliced or cut into 1/4-inch dice; zucchini, cut into 1-inch slices or sliced diagonally 1/4 inch thick.

BEEF

CORNED BEEF AND CABBAGE

Serves 4 to 6

1 4-pound corned beef brisket, soaked in cold
   water to cover for 2 hours to remove
   excess brine if necessary
1 bay leaf
6 peppercorns
1 onion, stuck with 2 cloves
1 carrot, sliced
1 celery rib, sliced
2 sprigs parsley
1 cup apple cider
6 carrots, halved crosswise
6 new potatoes
1 small head cabbage, cut into 4 to 6 wedges
accompaniments: Dijon-style mustard, horseradish,
   gherkin pickles

Top-of-the-Stove Method

Combine all ingredients in a soup pot except the halved carrots, potatoes and cabbage. Add enough water to cover. Bring to a rapid boil and skim off any surface scum. Lower heat, cover and simmer 1-1/2 hours or until tender. Remove corned beef to a platter and keep warm. Add halved carrots and the potatoes to pot and cook 15 minutes. Add cabbage and cook 15 minutes. Surround corned beef with vegetables. Serve with accompaniments.

Slow Cooker Method

Combine all ingredients, except cabbage, with water to cover and cook on low, covered, for 8 to 10 hours. Remove corned beef and vegetables to a platter and keep warm. Add cabbage to pot, cover and cook on high for 20 minutes. Place cabbage on platter with meat and vegetables. Serve with accompaniments.

Pressure Cooker Method

Place all ingredients except cabbage, halved carrots and potatoes in a pressure cooker with water to two-thirds capacity. Cover and bring to full pressure. When steam appears, reduce heat and cook on low 25 minutes. Reduce pressure completely, uncover and remove corned beef to a platter and keep warm. Add carrots and potatoes to pot, cover and cook 15 minutes, not under pressure. Add cabbage, cover and cook 15 minutes. Surround corned beef with vegetables. Serve with accompaniments.

MEATLOAF WITH POTATOES AND CHEESE FILLING

Serves 6
1 pound lean ground beef
1/2 pound ground veal
3/4 cup bread crumbs
1/2 cup grated Parmesan cheese
1/4 cup chopped parsley
1 onion, chopped
2 eggs
1/2 cup milk
1 teaspoon salt
1/2 teaspoon freshly ground pepper
3 tablespoons olive oil
2 cups mashed cooked potatoes
1/2 pound mozzarella or Monterey Jack cheese, sliced

Combine all ingredients except the oil, potatoes and sliced cheese and mix well. Place half of this mixture in a large loaf pan or baking dish which has been brushed with 1 tablespoon of the olive oil. Layer the potatoes and then the cheese on top of the meat mixture. Top with remaining meat mixture, covering potatoes and cheese completely. Brush top with the remaining oil and bake in a preheated 350° oven for 1 hour or until meat is brown on top, but not dry.

SWEET AND SOUR BEEF WITH FRUIT

Serves 4 to 6
3 onions, sliced
4 tablespoons butter
2 tomatoes, peeled, seeded and diced
1-1/2 pounds round steak, cut into
   1/2-inch dice, or
1-1/2 pounds lean ground beef
1 teaspoon salt
1/2 teaspoon freshly ground pepper
1 cup beef stock
2 pears, peeled and sliced
2 peaches, peeled and sliced, or
6 apricots, peeled and sliced
6 plums, peeled and sliced
3 potatoes, peeled and diced
3 tablespoons raisins
garnish: toasted slivered almonds

In a saucepan brown onions in butter; add tomatoes and cook for 2 minutes. Add beef and cook and stir for 2 minutes. Add salt, pepper and stock. Simmer, covered, for 30 minutes. Add fruit and potatoes and cook for 15 to 20 minutes or until potatoes are tender. Add raisins and serve garnished with almonds.

BEEF

CHILE CON CARNE

Serves 6 to 8

2 pounds stewing beef, cut into 1/2-inch cubes, or
1 pound each stewing beef and pork butt,
   cut into 1/2-inch cubes
1 onion, chopped
3 cloves garlic, minced
2 tablespoons lard
3 cups peeled and chopped ripe tomatoes
1/4 cup chili powder, mixed with
1 tablespoon flour
1 tablespoon minced oregano, or
1 teaspoon dried oregano
1/2 teaspoon ground cumin
2 bay leaves
1 teaspoon salt
1 cup pitted ripe olives
garnishes: chopped onions, minced fresh green
   chilies, chopped coriander
accompaniment: warm tortillas

Top-of-the-Stove Method
(Dutch oven or large skillet may be used)
Brown meat, onion and garlic in lard. Add tomatoes, chili powder-flour mixture, oregano, cumin, bay leaves and salt. Bring just to a boil, lower heat, cover and simmer for 2 hours. Add olives and simmer another 10 minutes. Garnish and serve with tortillas.

Slow Cooker Method
Brown the meat, onion and garlic in lard in a skillet or a slow cooker with a browning unit. Combine meat mixture and remaining ingredients except olives in a slow cooker. Cover and cook on low 6 to 8 hours. Add olives, cover and cook on high 10 minutes. Garnish and serve with tortillas.

Pressure Cooker Method

In a pressure cooker brown meat, onion and garlic in lard. Add the tomatoes, chili powder-flour mixture, oregano, cumin, bay leaves, salt and 1 cup water. Cover and bring to full pressure. When steam appears, reduce heat and cook on low for 25 minutes. Reduce pressure completely, uncover, add olives and cook 10 minutes, not under pressure. Garnish and serve with tortillas.

Wet Clay Cooker Method

Combine all ingredients except olives in a pre-soaked unglazed clay cooker. Cover and place in a cold oven. Turn oven to 400° and bake 1-1/2 hours. Remove from oven, add olives, cover and let stand 10 minutes. Garnish and serve with tortillas.

Note To prepare chile with beans, add 2 cups or more of cooked beans (pinto, pink or kidney beans) to the pot after prescribed cooking time and just heat through before serving.

BOILED BEEF SALAD

Serves 4

2 cups diced boiled beef
1 small onion, diced
1 cup diced celery
1 cup diced red or green bell pepper (or half and half)
1 cup diced cooked potatoes
1/2 cup chopped parsley
1 tablespoon Dijon-style mustard
1 teaspoon salt
1/2 teaspoon freshly ground pepper
1/3 cup olive oil
1/4 cup wine vinegar
lettuce leaves
2 tomatoes, cut into wedges
2 hard-cooked eggs, cut into quarters

Combine all ingredients, except for lettuce, tomatoes and eggs, and toss well. Place lettuce leaves on individual cold salad plates, spoon beef mixture on top and surround with tomatoes and eggs.

BEEF

RED FLANNEL HASH

Serves 4
1 medium-sized onion, chopped
6 tablespoons butter
3 medium-sized beets, cooked and diced
1 cup diced cooked potato
1 cup diced cooked corned beef or boiled beef
salt and freshly ground pepper to taste
2 tablespoons heavy cream

In a skillet sauté the onion in half the butter until transparent. Add the beets, potato and corned beef, stirring well to combine with the onion. Season with salt and pepper and cook over low heat for 10 minutes. Drizzle cream over the hash and dot with the remaining butter. Put under a pre-heated broiler for 5 minutes or until top is crusty and brown.

STUFFED CABBAGE, UKRAINIAN STYLE

Serves 4 to 6
1-1/2 pounds lean ground beef
1 cup cooked rice
1 teaspoon salt
1/2 teaspoon freshly ground pepper
8 to 10 large cabbage leaves, blanched
   until wilted
1 cup tomato sauce
1 6-ounce can tomato paste
1 onion, chopped
1/4 cup vinegar
1 cup water
2 tablespoons sugar
8 gingersnaps, crushed

Oven Method

Combine the meat, rice, salt and pepper. Fill each cabbage leaf with about 1/2 cup of the meat-rice mixture, fold in sides like an envelope, roll up and place seam side down in a shallow baking dish or casserole. Combine remaining ingredients and pour over cabbage rolls. Cover and bake in a preheated 325° oven for 1 hour.

Slow Cooker Method

Prepare stuffed cabbage rolls as directed for oven method. Place seam side down in a slow cooker. Combine remaining ingredients, reducing water to 3/4 cup, and pour over cabbage rolls. Cover and cook on low 6 to 8 hours.

BEEF

TRANSYLVANIA VEAL STEW

Serves 6 to 8

2 pounds boneless veal, cut into 1-inch cubes,
    dusted with
2 tablespoons flour
3 tablespoons each butter and corn oil
2 onions, finely chopped
3 potatoes, peeled and thinly sliced
2 zucchini, sliced
2 bell peppers, sliced
3 tablespoons chopped parsley
1 cup cut-up green beans
salt and freshly ground pepper to taste
1 pound ripe tomatoes, sliced
1 cup (1/2 pint) sour cream

Oven Method
Sauté veal in butter and oil in a large flameproof casserole until lightly browned. Add the onions and cook until browned. Remove from heat. Add potatoes, zucchini, bell peppers, parsley, green beans, salt and pepper. Top with sliced tomatoes. Cover and bake in a preheated 350° oven for 1 hour or until tender. Remove from oven and stir in sour cream.

Slow Cooker Method
Sauté veal in butter and oil in a skillet or a slow cooker with a browning unit. Add the onions and cook until browned. Put the potatoes in the bottom of a slow cooker. Add the browned meat, onions and remaining ingredients, except the sour cream, placing the tomatoes on top. Cover and cook on low 6 to 8 hours. Stir in sour cream when ready to serve.

STUFFED BREAST OF VEAL

Serves 6
1 3- to 4-pound breast of veal
1/2 cup chopped onion
3 tablespoons butter
1 crusty French bread roll, soaked in water,
    squeezed to remove excess water and crumbled
1/2 cup diced ham
1 cup cooked peas or asparagus tips
2 tablespoons chopped parsley
2 eggs, beaten
1 teaspoon salt
1/2 teaspoon freshly ground pepper
1 teaspoon paprika
1 cup tomato juice
1/2 cup sour cream

Make a pocket in the breast of veal. Sauté the onion in butter until transparent. Add the bread crumbs, ham, peas and parsley and blend well for 2 minutes. Remove from heat and mix the eggs into the bread mixture. Sprinkle the breast with salt, pepper and paprika inside and out. Stuff with bread mixture and sew up or skewer opening. Put in a roasting pan and roast in a preheated 325° oven for 1-1/2 hours or until meat is tender and brown. Baste occasionally with tomato juice. When veal is cooked, remove it from pan and add sour cream to pan juices, blending well. Slice veal and spoon sauce over slices.

LIVER DUMPLINGS

Serves 6
1-1/2 pounds calf or beef liver
1 large onion
3 tablespoons chopped chives
3 tablespoons chopped parsley
5 slices white bread, crusts removed
2 eggs
2 tablespoons flour
2 teaspoons salt
1/2 teaspoon freshly ground pepper
1/4 teaspoon freshly grated nutmeg
accompaniments:
    crisply cooked bacon
    sliced tomatoes or coleslaw

Grind liver with onion, chives, parsley and bread. Add eggs, flour, salt, pepper and nutmeg and mix well. Bring 2 quarts water to a boil in a large saucepan. Drop liver mixture by spoonfuls into boiling water, rinsing spoon in hot water each time. Cover pan and simmer for 10 minutes. Remove dumplings with slotted spoon and place on heated platter. Serve with accompaniments.

BEEF

BRAISED OXTAILS, SPANISH STYLE

Serves 6
3 to 4 pounds oxtails, disjointed
3 tablespoons olive oil
2 onions, chopped
2 cloves garlic, finely chopped
1 tablespoon flour
2 cups beef stock
1 cup dry red wine
1/2 cup tomato sauce
6 peppercorns
1/2 teaspoon dried oregano
1 dried red chili pepper, seeded and chopped
2 whole cloves
2 carrots, chopped
1 sweet red pepper, chopped
1 tablespoon chopped parsley
2 potatoes, peeled and cut into chunks
salt and freshly ground pepper to taste

Top-of-the-Stove Method
In a Dutch oven brown oxtails on all sides in oil. Add onions and garlic and cook 5 minutes. Sprinkle flour over the meat, blend well, and cook 2 minutes. Add stock, wine, tomato sauce, peppercorns, oregano, chili pepper and cloves. Cover and simmer 1-1/2 hours or until meat is almost tender. Add remaining ingredients and cook 20 minutes.

Slow Cooker Method
Brown oxtails on all sides in oil in a skillet or a slow cooker with a browning unit. Add onions and garlic and cook 5 minutes. Sprinkle flour over the meat, blend well and cook 2 minutes. Reduce stock to 1-1/2 cups and wine to 3/4 cup and add with all the remaining ingredients and the meat to a slow cooker, placing potatoes in the bottom. Cover and cook on low 8 to 10 hours.

Pressure Cooker Method

In a pressure cooker brown oxtails on all sides in oil. Add onions and garlic and cook 5 minutes. Sprinkle flour over the meat, blend well, and cook 2 minutes. Add stock, wine, tomato sauce, peppercorns, oregano, chili pepper, cloves and 1 cup water. Cover and bring to full pressure. When steam appears, reduce heat and cook on low 30 minutes. Reduce pressure completely, uncover, add remaining ingredients and cook 20 minutes, not under pressure.

Wet Clay Cooker Method

Sprinkle oxtails with flour. Place in a pre-soaked unglazed clay cooker and add onions, garlic, only 1-1/2 cups beef stock and 3/4 cup wine, tomato sauce, peppercorns, oregano, chili pepper and cloves. Cover and place in a cold oven. Turn oven to 400° and bake 1-1/2 hours. Add remaining ingredients, cover and bake 20 minutes. Remove from oven and let stand 10 minutes.

BEEF

CARIBBEAN OXTAIL STEW

Serves 6
3 pounds oxtails, disjointed
2 tablespoons corn oil
1 tablespoon chili powder
1 tablespoon dry mustard
1 tablespoon cornstarch
1 teaspoon salt
2 tablespoons fresh lemon juice
2 cups fresh orange juice
1/2 cup raisins
1 bell pepper, cut into strips
1 cup pitted ripe olives
3 celery ribs, thinly sliced
1 teaspoon freshly grated orange peel
garnish: watercress sprigs
accompaniment: freshly cooked rice

Top-of-the-Stove Method
In a Dutch oven brown the oxtails in the oil. Mix together the chili powder, mustard, cornstarch, salt and lemon and orange juices. Add mixture to the meat and bring just to a boil. Lower heat, cover and simmer 2 hours. Add raisins, bell pepper, olives and celery. Cover and cook 15 minutes. Stir in grated orange peel, garnish with watercress and serve over rice.

Slow Cooker Method
Brown the oxtails in the oil in a skillet or a slow cooker with a browning unit. Mix together chili powder, mustard, cornstarch, salt and lemon and orange juices, reducing the orange juice to 1-1/2 cups. Add to slow cooker with the oxtails, cover and cook on low 8 to 10 hours. Add raisins, bell pepper, olives and celery, cover, turn on high and cook 20 minutes. Stir in grated orange peel, garnish with watercress and serve over rice.

Pressure Cooker Method
In a pressure cooker brown the oxtails in the oil. Mix together the chili powder, mustard, cornstarch, salt and lemon and orange juices with 1 cup water. Add mixture to pressure cooker, cover and bring to full pressure. When steam appears, reduce heat and cook on low 30 minutes. Reduce pressure completely, uncover and add raisins, bell pepper, olives and celery. Cover and cook 15 minutes, not under pressure. Stir in grated orange peel, garnish with watercress and serve over rice.

Wet Clay Cooker Method
Place oxtails in a pre-soaked unglazed clay cooker. Combine oil, chili powder, mustard, cornstarch, salt and lemon and orange juices, reducing orange juice to 1-1/2 cups, and add to clay cooker. Cover and place in a cold oven. Turn oven to 400° and bake 1-1/2 hours. Add raisins, bell pepper, olives and celery, cover and bake 10 minutes. Remove from oven; let stand 10 minutes. Stir in orange peel, garnish and serve over rice.

BOILED TONGUE DINNER

Serves 6

1 beef tongue, about 3 pounds
1 pound marrow bones, cut into 1-1/2-inch pieces
1 clove garlic
1 onion, stuck with 2 cloves
1/2 teaspoon dried rosemary
1 bay leaf
1 teaspoon salt
1/2 teaspoon freshly ground pepper
6 turnips, cut into chunks
3 celery ribs, with some leaves
12 small boiling onions
6 new potatoes
6 whole leeks, white parts only
accompaniments: horseradish, Dijon-style mustard

Top-of-the-Stove Method

Combine tongue, marrow bones, garlic, onion, rosemary, bay leaf, salt, pepper and 3 quarts water in a large soup pot. Simmer for 1-1/2 hours. Add vegetables and cook 20 minutes or until vegetables are tender. Remove tongue from pot, let stand 10 minutes, skin and slice. Place on a warmed platter.

Remove vegetables and marrow bones from broth with a slotted spoon and place on platter with tongue. Serve with accompaniments. Broth may be strained and served separately.

Slow Cooker Method

Combine all ingredients with water to cover in a slow cooker, placing potatoes and turnips in the bottom. Cover and cook on low 8 to 10 hours. Remove tongue from pot and proceed as directed for top-of-the-stove method.

Pressure Cooker Method

Place the tongue, marrow bones, garlic, onion, rosemary, bay leaf, salt and pepper in a pressure cooker with water to two-thirds capacity. Cover and bring to full pressure. When steam appears, reduce heat and cook on low 20 minutes. Reduce pressure completely, uncover, add all remaining ingredients, cover and cook 30 minutes or until vegetables are tender, not under pressure. Let stand 10 minutes to blend flavors. Remove tongue from pot and proceed as directed for top-of-the-stove method.

BEEF

TONGUE STUFFED WITH HAM AND SAUSAGE

Serves 6 to 8

1 3- to 4-pound beef tongue
1/2 cup fresh lemon juice
1/2 pound ground veal
1/2 pound bulk pork sausage
1/2 cup minced ham
2 eggs, beaten
1-1/2 teaspoons salt
1/2 teaspoon freshly ground pepper
2 tablespoons chopped coriander or parsley
1/2 cup bread crumbs
1 teaspoon dried oregano
1 bay leaf
1 onion, quartered
6 peppercorns
1 teaspoon salt
1 cup dry white wine
2 cups peeled and diced ripe tomatoes
1/2 cup rice
accompaniment: Tomato Salsa, following

Top-of-the-Stove Method
Wash tongue and dry with paper towels. Make a deep slit the length of the underside almost to the tip. Make several lengthwise slashes in the flesh. Rub lemon juice into tongue and let stand 10 minutes. Make a forcemeat by combining the veal, sausage, ham, eggs, salt, pepper, coriander and bread crumbs. Pile onto tongue and truss sides of tongue together with heavy thread. Place stuffed tongue in a large soup pot with oregano, bay leaf, onion, peppercorns, salt, wine and water to cover (about 2 quarts). Cover and simmer for 2 hours. Remove tongue, reserving liquid. Let tongue stand 10 minutes, then skin and slice. Strain the reserved liquid and add tomatoes and rice. Simmer 20 minutes and serve as soup, either with tongue or as another course. Serve tongue with Tomato Salsa. (This dish is also delicious served cold.)

Slow Cooker Method
Prepare stuffed tongue as directed for top-of-the-stove method. Place the tongue with all ingredients except tomatoes and rice in a slow cooker, adding water to cover. Cover and cook on low 8 to 10 hours. Remove tongue and let stand 10 minutes; then skin and slice. Strain the cooking liquid and return to slow cooker. Add tomatoes and rice, cover and cook on high 20 minutes. Serve as directed for top-of-the-stove method.

TOMATO SALSA

Makes 1 pint
2 cups peeled and chopped ripe tomatoes
2 or more fresh green chili peppers,
    seeded and chopped
2 tablespoons olive oil
2 tablespoons red wine vinegar

1 small onion, finely chopped
1 clove garlic, finely chopped
1/2 teaspoon dried oregano
1 tablespoon chopped coriander
salt and freshly ground pepper to taste

Combine all ingredients and refrigerate for 2 to 3 hours to allow flavors to blend.

TRIPES A LA NORMANDY
(Tripe with Calf's Feet)

Serves 4 to 6
4 pounds honeycomb tripe, cut into 2-inch
    squares and blanched
2 calf's feet, blanched
2 cups dry white wine
1 quart beef stock, heated
2 onions, each stuck with 2 cloves
4 leeks, white parts only
2 cloves garlic
2 celery ribs, halved with some leaves
1 bay leaf
1/2 teaspoon dried thyme
1/4 cup chopped parsley
2 carrots, halved

1/2 pound button mushrooms
2 teaspoons salt
1 teaspoon freshly ground pepper
accompaniments:
    Dijon-style mustard
    boiled new potatoes or French bread

Combine all the ingredients in an earthenware or other large heatproof casserole. Cover with a tight-fitting lid and place in a preheated 325° oven for 4 hours or until meat is tender. Remove meat from calf's feet and return meat to the casserole. Continue cooking, uncovered, for 1 hour or until liquid has reduced to a saucelike consistency. Serve very hot with Dijon-style mustard and boiled new potatoes or French bread.

MEAL IN A DISH PASTRIES

PASTRY FOR TWO-CRUST PIE

Makes 2 8- or 9-inch crusts
2 cups unbleached white flour
1 teaspoon salt
3/4 cup shortening or lard, or half butter and
   half shortening
5 to 6 tablespoons cold water

Put the flour and salt in a bowl and cut in shortening with a pastry blender or two knives until mixture is crumbly. Sprinkle water over mixture, mixing lightly with a fork. Form into a ball with hands and divide in half. Roll out each half on lightly floured board to a thickness of 1/8 inch. Fit into pie plates or on top of pie according to recipe. For one crust, halve the above ingredients and proceed as directed.

BISCUIT PASTRY

Makes 1 10-inch crust
1-1/4 cups unbleached white flour
1 tablespoon baking powder
1/2 teaspoon salt
3 tablespoons butter
3 tablespoons corn oil
1 egg, beaten
cold water

Sift the flour, baking powder and salt together. Cut in butter with a pastry blender or 2 knives until mixture is crumbly. Add oil, egg and just enough cold water to form dough into a ball with hands. Roll out 1/4 inch thick. May be used for top crust of pot pies or deep-dish pies.

MEAL IN A DISH PASTRIES

CRAB QUICHE

Serves 4 to 6
half recipe Pastry for Two-Crust Pie, page 131
1/2 pound cooked flaked crab meat
1 cup grated Swiss cheese
3 eggs
1 cup heavy cream
3 tablespoons chopped chives
1/2 teaspoon salt
1/8 teaspoon white pepper
chopped fresh dill

Prepare 1 9-inch pie shell and prick all over with fork tines. Bake for 5 minutes in a preheated 350° oven. Remove crust from oven and turn oven to 375°. Sprinkle crab meat over crust and top with cheese. Mix together remaining ingredients except dill and pour mixture over crab and cheese. Sprinkle dill on top and bake in the preheated 375° oven for 30 to 35 minutes.

QUICHE LORRAINE

Serves 4 to 6
half recipe Pastry for Two-Crust Pie, page 131
6 thick slices bacon, cooked crisp, drained
   and crumbled
3 eggs
1 tablespoon flour
pinch of freshly grated nutmeg
1/4 teaspoon salt
1/8 teaspoon freshly ground pepper
1 cup half-and-half
2 tablespoons butter, melted

Prepare 1 9-inch pastry shell and prick all over with fork tines. Bake for 5 minutes in a preheated 350° oven. Remove crust from oven and turn oven to 375°. Distribute bacon pieces in pie shell. Beat together remaining ingredients and pour over bacon. Bake in a preheated 375° oven for 30 to 35 minutes or until custard is set and top is lightly browned. Serve warm.

VEAL PASTIES

Makes 8 pasties; serves 4
Pastry for Two-Crust Pie, page 131
1 pound ground veal
2 hard-cooked eggs, chopped
1/4 cup chopped pitted prunes
1/4 cup chopped pitted dates
3 tablespoons dried currants
3 tablespoons pine nuts or
   slivered blanched almonds
1/2 teaspoon fennel seeds
1/4 teaspoon each ground cinnamon and ginger
1/8 teaspoon freshly grated nutmeg

Prepare pastry dough and set aside. Combine all remaining ingredients for the filling and set aside. Divide the pastry dough into 8 equal portions and roll out each portion on a lightly floured board into a 6-inch round. Divide filling into 8 portions and place a portion on each pastry round. Fold over dough and crimp edges. Place pasties on a cookie sheet and bake in a preheated 375° oven for 25 minutes or until golden.

CORNISH PASTIES

Makes 8 pasties; serves 4
Pastry for Two-Crust Pie, page 131
1-1/2 pounds lean ground beef
1 potato, peeled and finely diced
1 onion, finely diced
1/2 cup chopped parsley
1 teaspoon salt
1/4 teaspoon freshly ground pepper

Prepare pastry dough and set aside. Combine all remaining ingredients for the filling and set aside. Divide the pastry dough into 8 equal portions and roll out each portion on a lightly floured board into a 6-inch round. Divide filling into 8 portions and place a portion on each pastry round. Fold over dough and crimp edges. Place pasties on a cookie sheet and bake in a preheated 375° oven for 25 minutes or until golden.

MEAL IN A DISH PASTRIES

SWISS CHEESE PIE

Serves 4 to 6
half recipe Pastry for Two-Crust Pie, page 131
1/2 pound imported Swiss cheese, grated
1 tablespoon flour
3 eggs, beaten
1 cup half-and-half
pinch of freshly grated nutmeg

Prepare 1 9-inch pastry shell and prick all over with fork tines. Bake for 5 minutes in a preheated 350° oven. Remove crust from oven and turn oven to 375°. Mix the cheese with the flour and spread evenly over the pie shell. Combine the eggs and cream and pour over cheese mixture. Grate some nutmeg on top and bake in a preheated 375° oven for 30 to 35 minutes or until center is set. Serve warm.

CHICKEN PIE

Serves 4 to 6
Pastry for Two-Crust Pie, page 131
melted butter
4 cups diced cooked chicken meat
salt and freshly ground pepper
1/4 teaspoon freshly grated nutmeg
3 eggs, beaten
1/2 cup dry white wine
1 cup cold rich chicken stock
4 hard-cooked eggs, chopped
1 cup coarsely chopped cooked artichoke
  hearts or asparagus tips
2 tablespoons chopped green onions

Prepare pastry dough and line a deep 9-inch pie plate with half the pastry. Brush with melted butter. Combine remaining ingredients, blending well, and pour into the pie shell. Roll out remaining dough and place on top, crimping edges. Make several slits in top of pastry and bake in a preheated 425° oven for 10 minutes. Lower heat to 325° and continue baking for 30 minutes or until golden. Serve hot or cold.

PORK AND APPLE PIE

Serves 4 or 5
Pastry for Two-Crust Pie, page 131
4 tart apples, peeled and sliced
1 pound lean ground pork
1/2 teaspoon dried thyme
1 tablespoon brown sugar
1/4 teaspoon powdered sage
1 teaspoon salt
1/4 teaspoon freshly ground pepper
2 tablespoons butter
1 egg, beaten with
1 teaspoon milk
accompaniments: freshly grated horseradish,
   sour cream

Prepare pastry dough and line a deep 9-inch pie plate with half the pastry. Combine the apples, pork, thyme, sugar, sage, salt and pepper and place mixture in pie shell; dot with butter. Roll out remaining dough and place on top, crimping edges. Make several slits in top of pastry. Brush with egg-milk mixture and bake in a preheated 400° oven for 1 hour. Serve at room temperature with accompaniments.

POTATO PIE

Makes 2 pies; serves 8 or more
Pastry for Two-Crust Pie, page 131
2 cups (1 pint) cottage cheese
2 cups unseasoned mashed potatoes
1/2 cup sour cream
3 eggs
1 teaspoon salt
1/8 teaspoon cayenne pepper
1/2 cup chopped green onions
1/2 cup grated Parmesan cheese

Prepare 2 9-inch pastry shells and set aside. Put cottage cheese through a sieve or whirl in a blender until smooth. Blend potatoes into cottage cheese and beat in sour cream, eggs, salt and cayenne. Stir in onions and Parmesan cheese. Spoon half of mixture into each pastry shell. Bake in a preheated 425° oven for 45 minutes or until golden.

Variation
For a Bacon-and-Potato Pie, add 6 slices bacon, crisply cooked and crumbled, to cottage cheese-potato mixture.

MEAL IN A DISH PASTRIES

EGGPLANT-AND-MACARONI PIE

Serves 6
Biscuit Pastry, page 131
1 small eggplant, peeled and cubed
2 tablespoons vinegar
1 onion, chopped
3 tablespoons olive oil
1/2 cup tomato paste
1/2 pound ground beef
2 chicken livers, parboiled 1 minute and minced
1/2 cup ricotta cheese or cream-style cottage cheese
1 teaspoon dried oregano
1/2 pound macaroni, cooked al dente
1/2 cup grated Monterey Jack cheese
1 hard-cooked egg, sliced
1 egg, beaten

Prepare pastry dough and set aside. Soak eggplant in water to cover and vinegar for 15 minutes; drain and pat dry. Sauté eggplant with onion in oil. Mix 1/2 cup water with tomato paste and add to eggplant mixture. Mix ground beef and chicken livers; add to eggplant mixture and simmer 5 minutes. Remove from heat, add ricotta and oregano and mix well. Layer half of macaroni, eggplant sauce and grated cheese in a buttered 2-quart casserole. Top with egg slices and repeat layers, ending with grated cheese. Pour beaten egg over all. Roll out pastry 1/4 inch thick and top casserole. Make several slits in top of pastry and bake in a preheated 375° oven for 45 minutes or until top is golden.

ROAST BEEF PIE

Serves 4
Biscuit Pastry, page 131
1/2 cup chopped onion
1 clove garlic, minced
1 cup thinly sliced mushrooms
1/4 cup minced bell pepper
3 tablespoons roast beef drippings or butter
3 tablespoons flour
1 teaspoon salt
1/2 teaspoon freshly ground pepper
pinch each of dried thyme, ground cloves and
    freshly grated nutmeg
2 cups beef stock
1 cup fresh peas (1 pound, unshelled)
1 cup sliced carrots
1 cup peeled and cubed potatoes
2 tablespoons chopped sweet pickle
1 tablespoon capers
2 cups cubed cooked roast beef

Prepare pastry dough and set aside. In a 2-quart flameproof casserole sauté the onion, garlic, mushrooms and bell pepper in drippings for 3 minutes. Sprinkle with flour and seasonings and cook over low heat until well blended. Add the stock and vegetables and cook 10 minutes or until vegetables are just tender. Remove from heat and add remaining ingredients. Roll out dough 1/4 inch thick and top casserole. Make several slits in top of pastry and bake pie in a preheated 425° oven for 30 minutes or until crust is golden.

KIDNEY-SAUSAGE-AND-VEGETABLE PIE

Serves 4
Biscuit Pastry, page 131
1 pound lamb or veal kidneys, suet removed
   and reserved
2 tablespoons flour
2 tablespoons butter
1/2 pound bulk pork sausage
1/4 teaspoon powdered sage
1/2 teaspoon dried marjoram
1/2 cup chopped onion
1/2 cup chopped celery with leaves
1 potato, peeled and diced
1 cup thinly sliced carrots
1 cup fresh peas (1 pound, unshelled)
1/2 cup water
1/4 cup dry sherry
1/2 teaspoon salt
1/4 teaspoon freshly ground pepper
1/8 teaspoon cayenne pepper

Prepare pastry dough and set aside. Mince enough of reserved suet to make 1 tablespoon. Slice kidneys and dust with the flour. Sauté kidneys in suet and butter in a 2-quart flameproof casserole. Add remaining ingredients, bring to a gentle boil, cover and simmer 20 minutes. Remove from heat. Roll out pastry dough 1/2 inch thick and top casserole with pastry, crimping edges. Make several slits in top of pastry and bake pie in a preheated 425° oven for 35 minutes or until top is golden.

SWEETBREAD-OYSTER PIE

Serves 4 to 6
Biscuit Pastry, page 131
1 pound sweetbreads, parboiled 2 minutes,
   drained and sliced 1/4 inch thick
1 pint oysters, drained and halved
2 hard-cooked eggs, sliced
2 cups freshly grated corn kernels
3 tablespoons butter
1-1/2 cups White Sauce, page 51
1/4 cup Madeira or dry sherry
1/4 teaspoon freshly grated nutmeg
1/8 teaspoon cayenne pepper
2 tablespoons chopped parsley
1/2 teaspoon salt
1/2 teaspoon white pepper

Prepare pastry dough and set aside. Layer sweetbreads, oysters, hard-cooked eggs and corn in a buttered 2-quart casserole. Combine remaining ingredients and pour over all. Roll out dough 1/4 inch thick and top casserole. Make several slits in pastry and bake pie in a preheated 375° oven for 1 hour or until golden.

PASTA, RICE & BEANS

COOKING PASTA

Serves 4 to 6
1 tablespoon salt
1 tablespoon cooking oil
1 pound fresh noodles, or
12 ounces dried noodles

Add salt and oil to 2 quarts water and bring to a boil. Gradually add noodles and cook over medium heat, stirring occasionally, approximately 3 minutes for fresh, 8 minutes for dried noodles. Cook until just tender (al dente). Serve with any of the following sauces.

Chinese Noodles One pound of fresh Chinese noodles or 1/2 pound dried Chinese noodles may be cooked by the above method.

ANCHOVY SAUCE

3/4 cup olive oil
2 cloves garlic, crushed
2 2-ounce cans anchovy fillets
4 fresh mint leaves, finely chopped
1/4 cup chopped parsley
2 tablespoons capers
10 pitted black olives, chopped
freshly ground pepper to taste

In a skillet heat oil and add garlic; sauté until garlic is brown and discard. Add anchovies to oil and cook, stirring until they dissolve into a paste. Remove from heat and blend in remaining ingredients. Toss with freshly cooked pasta and serve immediately.

PASTA, RICE & BEANS

TOMATO SAUCE, NEAPOLITAN STYLE

1 cup olive oil
3 cloves garlic, crushed
4 cups peeled, seeded and chopped ripe tomatoes
2 tablespoons chopped basil, or
2 teaspoons dried basil
2 tablespoons chopped parsley
salt and freshly ground pepper to taste

In a skillet heat oil and sauté garlic until brown; discard garlic and add tomatoes, basil, parsley, salt and pepper. Cook for 30 minutes over moderate heat. Toss with freshly cooked pasta and serve immediately.

OLIVE OIL, GARLIC AND CHILI SAUCE

1 cup olive oil
3 to 4 cloves garlic, minced
1 or more fresh green chili peppers, minced
1/4 cup chopped parsley
freshly ground pepper to taste

In a skillet heat oil and add garlic, chilies and parsley; simmer 5 minutes. Toss with freshly cooked pasta and season with pepper. Serve immediately.

BACON SAUCE

2 tablespoons olive oil
1/2 pound lean bacon, diced
1 onion, sliced
3 large ripe tomatoes, peeled and chopped
1 teaspoon dried marjoram
salt and freshly ground pepper to taste
1 cup grated Parmesan cheese

In a skillet heat oil and fry bacon over low heat until fat is rendered; add onion and cook until transparent. Add tomatoes and marjoram and season with salt and pepper. Bring to a simmer and cook for 10 minutes. Toss with freshly cooked pasta and sprinkle with cheese. Serve immediately.

SHRIMP AND TOMATO SAUCE

2 tablespoons olive oil
1 onion, chopped
2 cloves garlic, minced
4 cups peeled and chopped Italian plum tomatoes
1-1/2 pounds raw shrimp, shelled and deveined
1 tablespoon each chopped basil and Italian parsley
salt and freshly ground pepper to taste

Heat oil and sauté onion and garlic until limp. Add **tomatoes** and cook 15 minutes over medium heat. Add shrimp and basil and cook 5 to 7 minutes longer or until shrimp is just cooked through; do not overcook. Season with salt and pepper. Pour over freshly cooked pasta and serve immediately.

PESTO

1-1/2 cups firmly packed chopped basil
4 cloves garlic, finely minced
3 tablespoons minced Italian parsley
1/2 cup pine nuts or walnuts (optional)
1 cup olive oil (or half butter, melted)
1/2 teaspoon salt
3/4 cup grated Parmesan cheese
    (or half Romano)

Crush basil, garlic cloves, parsley and pine nuts with a mortar and pestle to form a paste. Gradually stir in olive oil, salt and Parmesan. Toss with freshly cooked pasta and serve immediately.

SHEPHERD'S NOODLES

1/2 pound Italian sausages
1 pound ricotta cheese (cream-style cottage cheese
    may be substituted)
1/2 cup milk
1/2 cup grated Parmesan cheese

Crumble the Italian sausages in a skillet and sauté until browned. Remove from heat and blend in ricotta and milk to form a thick sauce. Pour over freshly cooked pasta, sprinkle with cheese and serve immediately.

PASTA, RICE & BEANS

CLAM AND GARLIC SAUCE

1/2 cup olive oil
3 cloves garlic, minced
2 7-ounce cans baby clams, drained and
   minced (reserve liquor)
3 tablespoons minced parsley
salt and freshly ground pepper to taste

In a skillet heat the oil and sauté garlic 1 minute. Add the clam liquor and parsley and cook for about 10 minutes. Add clams and heat through. Season with salt and pepper. Pour sauce over freshly cooked pasta and serve immediately.

RED CLAM SAUCE

3 pounds baby clams in the shell, or
2 7-ounce cans baby clams, drained (reserve liquor)
2 cloves garlic (for clams in the shell)
1/2 cup olive oil
1 small onion, sliced
1/2 cup dry white wine
3 cups peeled, seeded and chopped ripe tomatoes
1 or more fresh green chili peppers, seeded
   and chopped (optional)
1/4 cup chopped parsley
salt and freshly ground pepper to taste

Soak baby clams in water to draw out sand. Wash thoroughly and put in a large pot with the garlic. Cover and cook over medium heat until clams open. Shell, reserving 1 cup liquor; set clams and liquor aside. Heat oil in a skillet and cook onion until browned. Add wine, tomatoes, reserved clam liquor and chilies. Cook over high heat for 20 minutes. Add reserved clams and the parsley. Season with salt and pepper and heat through. Pour over freshly cooked pasta and serve immediately.

CHICKEN LIVER AND MUSHROOM SAUCE

1 pound chicken livers, quartered and dusted with
    flour seasoned with salt and freshly ground
    pepper to taste
6 tablespoons olive oil
1 clove garlic, finely chopped
1 onion, chopped
1/2 pound mushrooms, chopped
2 cups peeled, seeded and chopped tomatoes
1 6-ounce can tomato paste
1 tablespoon chopped basil, or
1 teaspoon dried basil
1 teaspoon dried oregano
1/4 teaspoon ground cinnamon
salt and cayenne pepper to taste
1/2 cup dry red wine
grated Parmesan cheese

In a skillet sauté chicken livers in 3 tablespoons of
the olive oil. Remove from skillet and set aside.
Sauté garlic, onion and mushrooms in remaining
oil. Add remaining ingredients except cheese and
simmer for 1 hour, stirring occasionally. Mixture
should be smooth and slightly thickened. Return
livers to sauce and heat through. Pour over freshly
cooked pasta and sprinkle with cheese. Serve immediately.

SPAGHETTI WITH MARINARA SAUCE

3 tablespoons olive oil
1 cup minced onions
4 cloves garlic, finely minced
1/2 pound mushrooms, chopped
4 cups peeled and chopped ripe tomatoes
2 tablespoons chopped basil
1/2 teaspoon dried oregano
1 teaspoon salt
1/4 teaspoon ground cinnamon
1 teaspoon sugar
1/4 teaspoon freshly ground pepper
3 anchovy fillets, chopped (optional)
grated Parmesan cheese

In a skillet heat oil and sauté onions, garlic and
mushrooms until golden. Add tomatoes, basil,
oregano, salt, cinnamon, sugar and pepper and
cook for 10 minutes. Add anchovies and simmer 5
minutes. Toss with freshly cooked pasta and sprinkle with cheese. Serve immediately.

Variation with Italian Sausage Sauté 1/2 pound
Italian sausages, crumbled or sliced, with the
onions, garlic and mushrooms.

PASTA, RICE & BEANS

NOODLES WITH BROCCOLI AND COTTAGE CHEESE

Serves 4
1 cup (1/2 pint) cream-style cottage cheese
1 cup (1/2 pint) sour cream
2 cups chopped cooked broccoli
1/4 cup white wine
1/2 cup chopped green onions
1 teaspoon salt
1/2 teaspoon freshly ground pepper
1/2 teaspoon freshly grated nutmeg
1/2 pound egg noodles, cooked al dente
2 tablespoons grated Parmesan cheese
2 tablespoons butter

Combine all ingredients except noodles, Parmesan cheese and butter and mix thoroughly. Place noodles in a buttered 2-quart casserole. Pour cheese sauce over the top, sprinkle with Parmesan and dot with butter. Bake in a preheated 350° oven for 30 minutes and serve immediately.

LASAGNE WITH CHICKEN AND CHEESE

Serves 4
12 ounces lasagne noodles (about 12 strips),
   cooked al dente
2 cups minced cooked chicken
1 cup cooked chopped spinach
1/2 pound mozzarella cheese, grated
1/2 teaspoon aniseed, crushed
salt and freshly ground pepper to taste
3/4 cup chicken stock

Butter a shallow baking dish and arrange 3 strips of lasagne noodles on bottom. Sprinkle one-third each of the chicken, spinach, cheese and seasoning over noodles. Repeat layers twice. Pour chicken stock over mixture, cover with aluminum foil and bake in a preheated 375° oven for 20 minutes. Remove foil and brown top under a preheated broiler, if desired.

Variations Substitute for the chicken any of the following: turkey, ham, veal, pork, beef, sweetbreads, chicken livers, shrimp, crab, tuna, hard-cooked eggs.

CHOW MEIN
(Pan-Fried Noodles)

1 pound fresh Chinese noodles, or
1/2 pound dried Chinese noodles
approximately 6 tablespoons peanut oil

Cook noodles as directed in Cooking Pasta, page 139. Heat 4 tablespoons of the oil in a wok or skillet. When hot, add half of the noodles, spreading them out evenly. Reduce heat to medium and brown lightly. Gently turn noodles over, being careful not to break them up, and brown other side. Remove to heatproof plate and keep warm in the oven. Add oil to skillet as needed and repeat with remaining noodles. Remove to plate and keep warm until ready to use. These noodles may be tossed with any stir-fry dish.

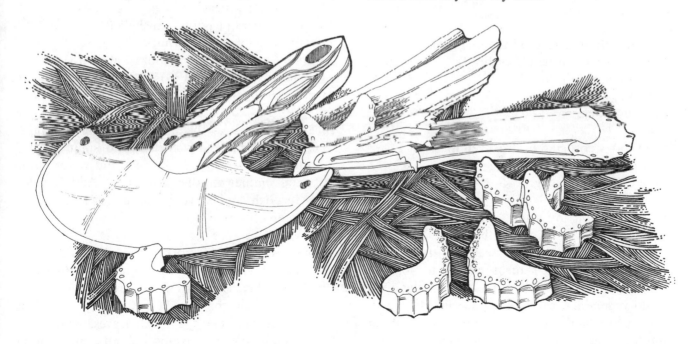

PASTA, RICE & BEANS

CHICKEN CHOW MEIN

Serves 4 to 6

3/4 pound boneless chicken breast meat, cut
   into thin strips
1 tablespoon soy sauce
2 teaspoons sherry
1/2 teaspoon sugar
4 tablespoons peanut oil
1 pound bean sprouts
1/2 cup sliced water chestnuts
1 celery rib, thinly sliced on the diagonal
1 cup matchstick-cut bamboo shoots
1 small onion, thinly sliced
1 teaspoon salt
1/2 teaspoon pepper
binder:
   2 teaspoons cornstarch, dissolved in
   2 tablespoons water
1 recipe Chow Mein, page 145

Combine chicken, soy sauce, sherry and sugar and
let stand 10 minutes. Heat 2 tablespoons of the oil
in a wok or skillet over high heat. Stir-fry chicken
1-1/2 minutes or until meat begins to lose its
pinkness. Remove to a plate. Heat remaining oil in
pan, add vegetables, salt and pepper and stir-fry 10
seconds. Cover and let steam rise to surface, about
2 minutes. Return chicken to pan, bind with cornstarch mixture and toss with noodles. Serve immediately.

SUEY MEIN
(Chicken and Shrimp Soup Noodles)

Serves 4 to 6

2 quarts chicken stock
3/4 pound boneless chicken breast meat, cut into
   thin strips or diced into bite-sized pieces
1/2 pound medium-sized shrimp, shelled
   and deveined
1/2 pound snow peas, or
1 cup fresh peas (1 pound, unshelled)
1/2 cup sliced water chestnuts
1 pound Chinese noodles, cooked al dente (see
   Cooking Pasta, page 139) and kept warm
garnish: chopped green onions (optional)

In a large pot heat the stock and bring to a rapid
boil. Lower heat, add chicken and simmer for 5
minutes. Add shrimp, snow peas and water chestnuts and simmer another 2 minutes. Add noodles,
heat through and serve in soup bowls garnished
with green onions.

Variations Raw beef, pork, lamb, chicken livers or
gizzards, or any combination may be substituted
for the chicken and shrimp, or cooked meats may
be added with the noodles. Coarsely cut Napa
cabbage or bok choy, spinach leaves, watercress,
thinly sliced carrots, bamboo shoots, mushrooms
or a combination of vegetables may be substituted
for the snow peas.

BEEF AND ASPARAGUS LO MEIN

Serves 4 to 6

1 pound flank or skirt steak, cut into thin strips
1 clove garlic, minced
1 onion, thinly sliced
2 tablespoons soy sauce
1 tablespoon sherry
1/2 teaspoon sugar
salt and pepper to taste
4 tablespoons peanut or corn oil
1 pound asparagus tips, sliced on the diagonal
   1/4 inch thick
binder:
   2 tablespoons cornstarch, dissolved in
   1/4 cup water
1 pound Chinese noodles, cooked al dente (see
   Cooking Pasta, page 139) and kept warm

Combine the meat, garlic, onion, soy sauce, sherry, sugar, salt and pepper. Heat 2 tablespoons of the oil in a wok or skillet and stir-fry the meat over high heat until it begins to lose its redness; do not overcook. Remove meat to a plate. Return pan to heat and heat remaining oil. Stir-fry the asparagus for 30 seconds. Add 1/2 cup water, cover and let steam rise to the surface, about 2 minutes. Return meat to pan and bind with cornstarch mixture, stirring well. Add noodles, toss together and serve immediately.

Variations Substitute cauliflower or broccoli flowerets, snow peas, green beans, sliced zucchini, coarsely cut bok choy, bean sprouts, chopped celery or bell pepper, or tomatoes cut into wedges for the asparagus. If using tomatoes, omit water when stir-frying vegetable. A combination of vegetables may also be used.

PASTA, RICE & BEANS

HAM, SHRIMP AND RICE

Serves 4
1/2 pound shrimp, shelled, deveined and cut in
   half lengthwise
1 cup diced ham
1 tablespoon soy sauce
1 tablespoon peanut oil
1 slice ginger root, minced (optional)
2 cups rice, washed and well drained
1 bell pepper, diced

Combine shrimp, ham, soy sauce, peanut oil and ginger root and let stand 10 minutes. Place rice in a 2-quart saucepan with a tight-fitting lid. Add 2-1/4 cups water, bring to a rapid boil and lower heat to medium. When all of the water and bubbles have disappeared from the surface of the rice, lower heat to simmer. Place shrimp and ham mixture on top of rice, cover and cook 15 minutes. Add the bell pepper, cover and cook 5 minutes. Serve immediately.

Variation Add 2 fresh bean-curd cakes, diced, the last 5 minutes of cooking.

CHICKEN AND RICE

Serves 4
1 pound boneless chicken, cut into thin strips
2 teaspoons sherry
1 tablespoon soy sauce
1 tablespoon peanut oil
1 or 2 slices ginger root, minced (optional)
2 cups rice, washed and well drained
1 cup fresh peas (1 pound, unshelled)

Combine chicken, sherry, soy sauce, peanut oil and ginger root and let stand 20 minutes. Place rice in a 2-quart saucepan with a tight-fitting lid. Add 2-1/4 cups water, bring to a rapid boil and lower heat to medium. When all of the water and bubbles have disappeared from the surface of the rice, lower heat to simmer. Place chicken mixture on top of rice, cover and cook 15 minutes. Add peas, cover and cook 5 minutes. Serve immediately.

Variations Omit peas and add 1 cup matchstick-cut bamboo shoots or half bamboo shoots and half water chestnuts the last 5 minutes of cooking. Sprinkle with 1/4 cup chopped green onions just before serving.

BEEF AND RICE

Serves 4
1 pound lean ground beef
1/2 cup minced water chestnuts
2 tablespoons soy sauce or oyster sauce
1 tablespoon sherry
1 clove garlic, minced
1 or 2 slices ginger root, minced (optional)
2 cups rice, washed and well drained
1/4 cup chopped green onions or coriander

Combine beef, water chestnuts, soy sauce, sherry, garlic and ginger root and let stand 10 minutes. Place rice in a 2-quart saucepan with a tight-fitting lid. Add 2-1/4 cups water, bring to a rapid boil and lower heat to medium. When all of the water and bubbles have disappeared from the surface of the rice, lower heat to simmer. Place beef mixture on top of rice, cover and cook 20 minutes. Mix in green onions and serve immediately.

Variations Add 1 cup chopped carrots or string beans to the beef mixture.

PORK AND BEAN STEW

Serves 6
1/4 cup olive oil
1 pound pork spareribs, cut into 3-inch lengths
1 pound Italian sausages
1 pound dried fava or lima beans, washed,
    soaked overnight and drained
1 small Savoy cabbage (about 1 pound), shredded
1 cup chopped fresh fennel with leaves
2 onions, thinly sliced
2 tomatoes, peeled and chopped
salt and freshly ground pepper to taste
accompaniments:
    crusty French or Italian bread
    grated Parmesan cheese

Heat oil in a flameproof casserole and fry spareribs until browned; add sausages and cook 5 minutes. Add beans, vegetables, salt, pepper and hot water to cover. Simmer for 1 hour or until beans are tender. Water may be added in small amounts as necessary. Serve hot with crusty bread and pass the grated cheese.

PASTA, RICE & BEANS

RED BEANS AND RICE

Serves 6

1 ham bone, cracked (so marrow will be released during cooking)
1 pound small dried red beans, washed, soaked overnight and drained
1 onion, chopped
3 cloves garlic, minced
salt and freshly ground pepper to taste
6 cups freshly cooked rice
1 cup chopped green onions

**Top-of-the-Stove Method
(Dutch oven, soup pot or large saucepan
may be used)**
Place ham bone in a pot with 2 quarts water. Bring to a boil and skim any surface scum. Add beans, onion and garlic. Reduce heat, cover and simmer for 2 hours or until beans are tender. Extra water may be added as needed during cooking period. Remove ham bone and mash some of the beans against the side of the pot to thicken the remaining liquid. Remove meat from the bone and return meat to the pot. Season with salt and pepper and serve with rice, topped with chopped green onions.

Slow Cooker Method
Place beans in bottom of a slow cooker and add remaining ingredients, except rice and green onions, with 1-1/2 quarts water. Cover and cook on high 2 hours. Turn heat to low and cook, covered, 10 to 12 hours. Proceed as directed for top-of-the-stove method.

Pressure Cooker Method
Combine all ingredients except rice and green onions, adding 2-1/2 quarts of water or not more than two-thirds capacity. Cover and bring to full pressure. When steam appears, reduce heat and cook on low 20 minutes. Reduce pressure completely and let stand, covered, 10 to 15 minutes to blend flavors. Proceed as directed for top-of-the-stove method.

MEXICAN POT BEANS

Serves 6

1 pound pinto or pink beans, washed, soaked
    overnight and drained
2 tablespoons lard or bacon drippings
1 small onion, chopped
1 tablespoon chopped oregano, or
1 teaspoon dried oregano
salt to taste
accompaniments: tortillas, chopped onions
    and chilies, grated Monterey Jack cheese,
    shredded lettuce, radishes

Top-of-the-Stove Method

Combine beans with lard, onion, oregano and 1-1/2 quarts water in a soup pot. Bring to a rapid boil, lower heat, cover and simmer 1 hour or until beans are tender. Add salt at end of cooking time. There should be a generous amount of broth left in the pot. Serve with accompaniments.

Slow Cooker Method

Combine all ingredients, except salt, with 3 cups water in a slow cooker. Cook on high, covered, 2 hours. Turn heat to low and cook, covered, 8 to 10 hours. Season with salt and serve with accompaniments.

Pressure Cooker Method

Place all ingredients, except salt, with 2 quarts water in a pressure cooker. Cover and bring to full pressure. When steam appears, reduce heat and cook on low 15 minutes. Reduce pressure completely and let stand, covered, 10 to 15 minutes to blend flavors. Season with salt and serve with accompaniments.

Refried Beans

Take as many of the cooked pot beans as desired with some of their broth and mash to a thick consistency (like mashed potatoes). Heat a heavy skillet over high heat, adding about 2 tablespoons of lard or corn oil for every cup of mashed beans. Fry the beans, scraping the bottom and sides frequently to integrate crusty bits with the whole. If desired, add some grated Monterey Jack cheese to the beans. Cover, lowering heat to medium and let cheese melt through (about 5 minutes).

PASTA, RICE & BEANS

HAM HOCKS AND LIMA BEANS

Serves 6
1 pound dried lima beans, washed, soaked overnight
  and drained
4 ham hocks, halved
2 bay leaves
1 onion, chopped
1 bell pepper, chopped
2 cups peeled and chopped ripe tomatoes
1 cup tomato sauce
1 teaspoon sugar
1/4 teaspoon ground cloves
1/2 teaspoon freshly ground pepper
salt to taste

Top-of-the-Stove Method
Combine beans and 2 quarts water in a large soup
pot with remaining ingredients. Cover and simmer
1-1/2 hours or until beans and meat are tender.

Slow Cooker Method
Place beans in the bottom of a slow cooker and
add remaining ingredients with 1-1/2 quarts water.
Cover and cook on high 2 hours. Turn heat to low
and cook, covered, 10 to 12 hours.

Pressure Cooker Method
Combine all ingredients, adding 2-1/2 quarts water
or not more than two-thirds capacity. Cover and
bring to full pressure. When steam appears, reduce
heat and cook on low 15 minutes. Reduce pressure
completely and let stand, covered, 10 to 15 minutes to blend flavors.

BEANS WITH TUNA

Serves 6
1/3 cup olive oil
1 clove garlic, crushed
1 pound small dried white beans, washed,
 soaked overnight and drained
2 cups peeled and chopped ripe tomatoes
2 6-1/2-ounce cans white tuna, drained and
 separated into chunks
2 sprigs basil, finely chopped
salt and freshly ground pepper to taste

Top-of-the-Stove Method

In a Dutch oven heat oil and sauté garlic until brown; discard garlic. Add beans and 2 quarts water, bring to a boil, reduce heat and simmer, covered, for 1-1/2 hours or until beans are tender. Add tomatoes, tuna, basil, salt and pepper. Simmer for 20 minutes and serve immediately.

Slow Cooker Method

Sauté garlic in oil until brown in a skillet or a slow cooker with a browning unit; discard garlic. Combine oil with beans and 1-1/2 quarts water in a slow cooker. Cover and cook on high 2 hours. Turn heat to low, cover and cook 8 hours. Add remaining ingredients, cover and cook on high for 30 minutes.

PASTA, RICE & BEANS

LAMB SHANKS, SAUSAGES AND BEANS

Serves 4 to 6
2 onions, chopped
3 tablespoons butter
1 pound small dried white beans,
   washed, soaked overnight and drained
3 lamb shanks
4 carrots, sliced
salt and freshly ground pepper to taste
1 bay leaf
4 garlic sausages, sliced diagonally 1/2 inch thick

Top-of-the-Stove Method
In a Dutch oven sauté onions in butter until transparent. Add remaining ingredients, except sausages, with 2 quarts water. Bring to a boil, lower heat, cover and simmer 1-1/2 hours or until meat and beans are tender. Add sausages and simmer 20 minutes longer.

Slow Cooker Method
Place beans in bottom of a slow cooker and add remaining ingredients except sausages, with 1-1/2 quarts water. Cover and cook on high 2 hours. Turn heat to low and cook, covered, 10 to 12 hours. Add sausages, cover and cook on high 20 minutes.

Pressure Cooker Method
In a pressure cooker sauté onions in butter until transparent. Add remaining ingredients except carrots and sausages, with 2-1/2 quarts water or not more than two-thirds capacity. Cover and bring to full pressure. When steam appears, reduce heat and cook on low 15 minutes. Reduce pressure completely, uncover, add carrots and sausages, cover and simmer 20 minutes, not under pressure.

PORK AND BEANS IN CREAM

Serves 6 to 8
1/2 pound salt pork, well rinsed and diced
1 onion, chopped
3 tablespoons butter
1 pound pink or kidney beans, washed, soaked
  overnight and drained
1 celery rib, chopped
1 bay leaf
1 cup heavy cream
2 egg yolks, beaten
salt and freshly ground pepper to taste
1/4 teaspoon freshly grated nutmeg
garnish: chopped parsley

Top-of-the-Stove Method
In a large pot sauté the salt pork and onion in
butter for 5 minutes. Add the beans, celery and
bay leaf with 2 quarts water. Bring to a boil,
skimming off any surface scum. Cover with a
tight-fitting lid, lower heat and simmer 1-1/2 hours
or until beans are tender. Combine cream, egg
yolks, salt, pepper and nutmeg and add to beans.
Simmer for 5 minutes or until thickened. Sprinkle
with parsley and serve.

Slow Cooker Method
Sauté the salt pork and onion in butter in a skillet
or a slow cooker with a browning unit for 5 minutes. Combine with the beans, celery and bay leaf
and 1-1/2 quarts water in a slow cooker. Cover
and cook on high 2 hours. Turn heat to low and
cook, covered, 10 to 12 hours. Combine cream, egg
yolks, salt and pepper and nutmeg and add to pot.
Cook on high, uncovered, 5 minutes or until thickened. Sprinkle with parsley and serve.

Pressure Cooker Method
In a pressure cooker sauté the salt pork and onion
in butter for 5 minutes. Add the beans, celery, bay
leaf and 2-1/2 quarts water or not more than
two-thirds capacity. Cover and bring to full pressure, reduce heat and cook on low 15 minutes.
Reduce pressure completely and let stand, covered,
10 to 15 minutes to blend flavors. Combine cream,
egg yolks, salt, pepper and nutmeg and add to
beans. Simmer, uncovered and not under pressure,
5 minutes or until thickened. Sprinkle with parsley
and serve.

PASTA, RICE & BEANS

MIXED MEATS WITH BLACK BEANS

Serves 8
1 pound black beans, washed, soaked overnight
  and drained
1 3-pound piece boneless beef brisket or pork
  butt (or a combination)
1/2 pound salt pork, well rinsed
1 bay leaf
1 teaspoon dried oregano
2 cloves garlic, minced
1 onion, chopped
1 or more dried red chili peppers
1/2 pound chorizo sausages
garnish:
    orange slices
    1 tablespoon grated orange rind
accompaniments:
    warm tortillas or French bread
    Tomato Salsa, page 129

Top-of-the-Stove Method
Combine all ingredients except chorizo in a large soup pot with 2 quarts water. Bring to a boil, lower heat, cover and simmer 1-1/2 hours or until beans are tender. Extra water may be added as needed during cooking period. Add chorizo and cook 20 minutes. Remove meats and keep warm. Mash some of the beans against the side of the pot to thicken the remaining liquid. Place beans in center of warmed platter. Slice meats and surround beans. Garnish with orange slices and grated rind. Serve with tortillas or bread and Tomato Salsa.

Slow Cooker Method
Place beans in bottom of a slow cooker and bury the salt pork in the beans. Add remaining ingredients except chorizo, with 1-1/2 quarts water. Cover and cook on high 2 hours. Turn heat to low and cook, covered, 10 to 12 hours. Add chorizo and cook, covered, on high 25 minutes. To serve proceed as directed for top-of-the-stove method.

Pressure Cooker Method
Combine all ingredients except chorizo, adding 2-1/2 quarts water or not more than two-thirds capacity. Cover and bring to full pressure. When steam appears, reduce heat and cook on low 15 minutes. Reduce pressure completely, uncover, add chorizo, cover and cook 20 minutes, not under pressure. To serve, proceed as directed for top-of-the-stove method.

OXTAILS AND GARBANZOS, ITALIAN STYLE

Serves 4 to 6
2 cloves garlic, finely chopped
1 onion, chopped
3 tablespoons olive oil
3 pounds oxtails, disjointed, parboiled 5
   minutes and drained
2 cups beef stock
1 cup chopped fresh fennel, including tops
1/2 teaspoon dried oregano
salt and freshly ground pepper to taste
1 cup diced cooked ham
2 cups cooked garbanzo beans
accompaniment: tossed green salad

Top-of-the-Stove Method
(Dutch oven or flameproof casserole may be used)
Sauté garlic and onion in olive oil until onion is transparent. Add oxtails and cook until browned. Add stock, fennel, oregano, salt and pepper. Cover and simmer 1-1/2 hours or until tender. Add ham and garbanzo beans and cook 20 minutes. Serve with a green salad.

Slow Cooker Method
Sauté the garlic and onion in oil in a skillet or a slow cooker with a browning unit. Add oxtails and cook until browned. Combine all ingredients except ham and garbanzos in a slow cooker, cover and cook on low 8 to 10 hours. Add ham and garbanzo beans, cover and cook on high 20 minutes. Serve with a green salad.

Pressure Cooker Method
In a pressure cooker sauté the onion and garlic in oil until onions are transparent. Add oxtails and cook until browned. Add all remaining ingredients except ham and garbanzos, adding 1 cup water. Cover and bring to full pressure. When steam appears, reduce heat and cook on low 30 minutes. Reduce pressure completely and add ham and garbanzos. Cover and cook for 20 minutes, not under pressure. Serve with a green salad.

Wet Clay Cooker Method
Combine all ingredients except ham and garbanzos, reducing stock to 1-1/2 cups. Place in a pre-soaked unglazed clay cooker, cover and place in a cold oven. Turn oven to 400° and bake 1-1/2 hours or until tender. Add ham and garbanzo beans, cover and bake 20 minutes. Remove from oven and let stand 10 minutes. Serve with a green salad.

TABLETOP COOKERY

One-pot cookery achieves its most festive form in tabletop cooking. For entertaining, these recipes are a boon to the otherwise harassed hostess/cook. With a hibachi, chafing dish or fondue pot she may now feed her guests without leaving the table.

True tabletop cooking was more widely practiced in the Orient than in Europe. The Chinese actually invented the hibachi, though it is now more associated with Japanese cooking in numerous grilled teriyaki dishes and the nabemono (meal in a pot) tradition. A version of this tableside grill can be found, however, in every country in the Orient in one guise or another. Another useful, although esoteric, tabletop cooking vessel is the Oriental firepot, which is designed to hold the hot charcoal within the pot.

Europe's contributions to tabletop cookery are the chafing dish and fondue pot. Classically these were used as warming dishes, rather than actual cooking pots. (The French term for chafing dish is *réchaud,* to re-warm.) In turn-of-the-century America, restaurant chefs began competing for dramatic dishes cooked and often flambéed at the table. By mid-century a chafing dish was virtually a staple in every middle-class household, only to be displaced by the fondue craze of the 1960's.

You don't, however, need specialized pots for tabletop cookery. An electric skillet or a skillet placed over a hot plate may be used in place of a firepot, fondue pot or chafing dish.

TABLETOP COOKERY

SHRIMP AND RICE

Serves 4
3 tablespoons butter
1 onion, chopped
1 fresh green chili pepper, seeded and minced
1/2 cup chopped bell pepper
1/4 cup chopped parsley
1 cup peeled and chopped ripe tomatoes
1 cup long-grain rice
1 pound medium-sized shrimp, shelled and
   deveined
1 cup diced cooked ham
garnish: 1/2 cup chopped green onions

Heat butter in the top pan (blazer) of a chafing dish placed directly over the flame and sauté onion, chili pepper and bell pepper until vegetables are limp. Add parsley and tomatoes, bring to a boil, then add rice and 1 cup hot water. Return to boil and stir in shrimp and ham. Cover, place top pan over the hot water pan (lower pan) and let steam 20 minutes or until rice is tender. Garnish with green onions.

SHRIMP NEWBURG

Serves 4 to 6
2 shallots, minced
4 tablespoons butter
1-1/2 pounds medium-sized shrimp, shelled
   and deveined
1/2 teaspoon paprika
pinch of cayenne pepper
1/2 cup Madeira or sherry
1-1/2 cups half-and-half
4 egg yolks, well beaten
1 tablespoon cognac
salt and white pepper to taste
garnish: 2 tablespoons minced parsley
accompaniment: freshly cooked rice or
   freshly made toast

In the top pan (blazer) of a chafing dish placed directly over a low flame, sauté the shallots in butter for 1 minute. Add the shrimp and cook over a brisk fire until shrimp become pink, about 3 minutes. Add paprika, cayenne and Madeira and cook until wine is reduced by half. Place the top pan over the hot water pan (lower pan). Blend half-and-half with egg yolks and gradually add to shrimp mixture. Stirring constantly to prevent curdling, cook until thickened. Add cognac, salt and pepper. Garnish with parsley and serve over rice or toast.

SHELLFISH STEW, CHILEAN STYLE

Serves 6
6 tablespoons butter
1 onion, chopped
4 tablespoons flour
1 quart fish stock or clam juice, heated
2 cups dry white wine
1/2 teaspoon white pepper
1 pound medium-sized shrimp, shelled, deveined
    and halved lengthwise
1 pound scallops, halved or quartered
1 or more fresh green chili peppers, seeded and
    minced
1 cup heavy cream
2 hard-cooked eggs, chopped
1/2 cup slivered blanched almonds
salt and freshly ground pepper to taste
accompaniment: crusty French rolls

Heat butter in the top pan (blazer) of a chafing dish placed directly over the flame and sauté onion until transparent. Blend in flour and cook 2 minutes. Add stock, wine and white pepper and simmer 20 minutes. Then add shrimp, scallops and chili peppers and cook 5 to 7 minutes or until seafood is done. Add cream and eggs; heat through. Stir in almonds, salt and pepper. Accompany with French rolls.

CAPE COD FISH CHOWDER

Serves 6
1/4 pound salt pork, well rinsed and diced
2 onions, thinly sliced
4 cups peeled and diced potatoes
1 celery rib with leaves, diced
2 pounds cod, halibut or other firm white fish
    fillets, cut into 1-inch pieces
2 cups milk
salt and freshly ground pepper to taste
2 tablespoons butter
accompaniment: pilot or soda crackers

In the top pan (blazer) of a chafing dish placed directly over the flame, sauté salt pork until fat is rendered. Add onions and cook until transparent; then add potatoes, celery and 4 cups boiling water. Cover and cook 10 minutes; add fish and cook 10 minutes. Add milk, salt, pepper and butter, heat through and serve with crackers.

Oyster and Corn Chowder
Omit fish and add 1 quart oysters with liquor. Reduce potatoes to 2 cups and add 2 cups freshly grated corn kernels.

TABLETOP COOKERY

EGGS RANCHEROS

Serves 4 to 6
2 tablespoons olive oil
1 clove garlic, minced
1 onion, chopped
1 or more fresh green chili peppers, seeded and
    chopped
2 cups peeled, seeded and chopped ripe tomatoes
1/2 teaspoon dried oregano
1/4 teaspoon ground cumin
6 eggs
accompaniment: warm tortillas or freshly made
    toast

Heat the oil in the top pan (blazer) of a chafing dish placed directly over the flame and sauté garlic and onion until transparent. Add chilies, tomatoes, oregano and cumin and bring to a boil. Break eggs one at a time onto a saucer, slip into tomato mixture and poach 3 minutes or until whites are set. Yolks should remain soft. Serve with tortillas or toast.

ASPARAGUS FRITTATA

Serves 4
3 tablespoons olive oil
1 clove garlic, finely minced
1 onion, thinly sliced
1 pound asparagus tips, thinly sliced on the
    diagonal
1/2 teaspoon dried oregano
1/2 teaspoon salt
1/4 teaspoon freshly ground pepper
6 eggs, beaten
1/2 cup grated Parmesan cheese
accompaniment: Italian bread

Heat oil in the top pan (blazer) of a chafing dish placed directly over the flame and sauté garlic and onion until transparent. Add asparagus and oregano, cover and cook 3 minutes or until asparagus are tender-crisp. Add salt and pepper to eggs and pour over asparagus, stirring once. When eggs begin to set, sprinkle cheese on top. Slip out onto a platter and cut into wedges. Serve with crusty Italian bread.

FETTUCCINE

Serves 4 to 6
1/4 pound butter
1-1/2 cups half-and-half
1 pound fresh fettuccine noodles or egg noodles,
    cooked al dente and kept warm
1-1/2 cups grated Parmesan cheese (or half
    Romano cheese)
freshly grated nutmeg
salt and freshly ground pepper to taste
accompaniments: antipasto platter composed of
    any combination of the following: anchovy
    fillets, Italian salami, marinated mushrooms or
    artichokes, cherry tomatoes, celery sticks,
    olives, mild pepperoni, radishes, etc.

In the top pan (blazer) of a chafing dish placed
directly over the flame, heat butter and half of the
half-and-half. Bring just to a boil, add noodles,
tossing lightly with a pair of forks. Sprinkle in
cheese and continue to toss noodles, gradually adding remaining cream. Add nutmeg, salt and pepper
and serve immediately.

SCRAMBLED EGGS AND SMOKED SALMON

Serves 4
6 eggs
3 tablespoons half-and-half
3 tablespoons chopped chives
3 tablespoons butter
8 slices smoked salmon (lox)
4 bagels, split and buttered, or
8 slices buttered rye toast

Beat together eggs, half-and-half and chives. Melt
butter in top pan (blazer) of a chafing dish placed
directly over the flame. Add egg mixture and stir
until eggs begin to set; do not overcook. Place a
slice of salmon on each bagel half or piece of toast
and top with scrambled eggs. Serve immediately.

TABLETOP COOKERY

BEER SAUSAGES

Serves 4
1 pound pork sausage links
1 cup beer
accompaniments:
    tart crisp apples, sliced, or
    pickles and sliced tomatoes
    rye bread and butter
    beer to drink

Prick sausages and cook until brown in the top pan (blazer) of a chafing dish placed directly over the flame. Pour off all drippings and add beer and continue cooking until beer has been reduced by half. Serve with accompaniments.

WELSH RABBIT

Serves 4 to 6
2 tablespoons butter
1 pound Cheddar cheese, grated
1 cup beer or ale, at room temperature
1/2 teaspoon paprika
1/2 teaspoon dry mustard
freshly made toast

Melt the butter in the top pan (blazer) of a chafing dish placed over hot water pan (lower pan). Add the cheese; when it begins to melt, slowly add the beer or ale, stirring constantly. Season with paprika and mustard and cook for 5 minutes. Lower heat and keep warm until ready to serve over hot toast.

CHILI RABBIT

Serves 6

3 tablespoons butter
1 small onion, minced
1 clove garlic, minced
1 or more fresh green chili peppers, seeded and
   chopped
2 tablespoons flour
1 cup milk
2 cups grated Cheddar cheese
1-1/2 cups peeled and chopped tomatoes
1/2 teaspoon salt
1/4 teaspoon freshly ground pepper
2 egg yolks, well beaten
accompaniment: crisp corn tortilla chips or
   French bread toast

Melt the butter in the top pan (blazer) of a chafing dish placed directly over a low flame and sauté the onion, garlic and chilies until onion is transparent. Place the top pan over hot water pan (lower pan), add the flour and blend well. Gradually add the milk, stirring constantly until smooth and thickened. Add the cheese and continue stirring until melted. Add tomatoes, salt and pepper and cook for 10 minutes. Blend 1/2 cup of the hot mixture with the egg yolks and return to the pan. Continue cooking and stirring for 2 minutes. Serve with tortilla chips or toasted French bread.

Variation Add 2 cups diced cooked chicken to the sauce when adding egg yolks.

TABLETOP COOKERY

BAGNA CAUDA

Serves 4
1/4 pound butter
1/2 cup olive oil
4 cloves garlic, minced
1 2-ounce can anchovy fillets, chopped
6 celery ribs, cut into sticks
3 bell peppers, cut into wide strips
4 medium-sized artichokes, cooked
1 cauliflower, broken into flowerets
3 zucchini, cut into sticks
8 green onions
8 whole mushrooms
6 fennel stalks
accompaniment: Italian or French bread

Heat butter and oil in the top pan (blazer) of a chafing dish placed directly over the flame and sauté garlic; do not brown. Remove from heat and add anchovies, stirring well. Return pan to low heat and continue cooking until anchovies have dissolved into a paste. Serve vegetables on individual plates for dipping into garlic-anchovy sauce. Accompany with Italian or French bread.

CURRY OF LAMB

Serves 4
2 tablespoons butter
1/4 cup chopped onion
1 tart apple, peeled and chopped
1 tablespoon flour
1 tablespoon curry powder
2 cups lamb or chicken stock
1 egg yolk, beaten
1 tablespoon fresh lemon juice
2 cups diced cooked lamb
salt and freshly ground pepper to taste
accompaniment:
    freshly cooked rice
    chutney, chopped toasted cashews

Melt butter in top pan (blazer) of a chafing dish placed directly over the flame and sauté onion and apple over a brisk fire until golden. Add flour and curry powder and cook 2 minutes. Stir in stock and cook until smooth and thickened, about 5 minutes. Reduce flame to low, remove 1/2 cup of the sauce and combine with egg yolk and lemon juice. Return to pan, add lamb, season with salt and pepper and heat through. Serve immediately with rice and accompaniments.

Variation Substitute 2 cups cooked shrimp for the lamb and use chicken stock.

MEATBALL CURRY

Serves 6 to 8
Meatballs
1 pound ground lamb
1/2 pound ground veal
1 onion, minced
1 egg, beaten
1 teaspoon salt
1/2 teaspoon freshly ground pepper
2 tablespoons chopped coriander or parsley

Sauce
3 tablespoons butter
1 onion, thinly sliced
3 tablespoons flour
1 tablespoon curry powder
2 teaspoons sugar
1 quart tomato juice
pinch of cayenne pepper

accompaniments:
    freshly cooked rice
    chutney
    chopped roasted peanuts
    minced green onions

Combine all the ingredients for meatballs and make walnut-sized balls. Set aside. For the sauce, heat butter in the top pan (blazer) of a chafing dish placed directly over the flame and sauté onion until transparent. Blend in flour and curry powder and cook 2 minutes. Add sugar, tomato juice and cayenne, stirring until slightly thickened. Add meatballs and cook 20 minutes. Serve over rice with accompaniments.

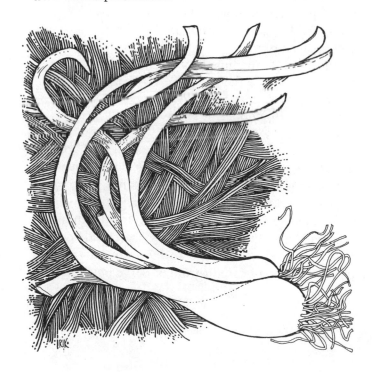

TABLETOP COOKERY

CHICKEN AND OYSTER MEDLEY, SOUTHERN STYLE

Serves 4 to 6
2 slices bacon, diced
2 tablespoons butter
2 cups diced cooked chicken
2 tomatoes, peeled, seeded and chopped
1 small onion, chopped
1 bell pepper, chopped
1 cup freshly grated corn kernels
1 cup sliced okra
1 cup small young lima beans
pinch of cayenne pepper
1 pint oysters, with their liquor
salt and white pepper to taste

In the top pan (blazer) of a chafing dish placed directly over the flame, sauté the bacon until the fat is rendered but the bacon is not crisp. Add butter, chicken, all the vegetables and the cayenne. Cover the chafing dish and cook for 10 minutes. Uncover and add the oysters; salt and pepper lightly. Cover and cook for 7 minutes or until oysters are just heated through. Serve immediately.

BARBECUED BEEF

Serves 6
3 tablespoons bacon drippings
3 onions, thinly sliced
2 cloves garlic, minced
2 celery ribs with leaves, finely chopped
1 teaspoon dry mustard
1 teaspoon chili powder
3 tablespoons brown sugar
1 teaspoon salt
1/2 teaspoon freshly ground pepper
1/4 cup vinegar
1/2 cup dry white wine
2 cups tomato juice
cooked roast beef, cut into thin strips to
  make 4 cups
garnish: chopped green onions (optional)
accompaniment: buns or freshly made toast

Heat bacon drippings in the top pan (blazer) of a chafing dish placed directly over the flame and sauté onions and garlic until transparent. Add celery and cook 5 minutes. Add remaining ingredients, except beef, place top pan over hot water pan (lower pan) and simmer for 25 minutes. Add beef and heat through, about 5 minutes. Serve garnished with green onions on buns or toast.

Variations Substitute cooked venison, roast pork, chicken or turkey for the roast beef.

SAUTÉED CHICKEN LIVERS AND BACON

Serves 4 to 6
3 slices bacon, diced
1 pound chicken livers, dredged in
2 tablespoons flour
1/4 cup chopped onion
1/4 cup chopped bell pepper
1/2 teaspoon dried tarragon
1/2 cup dry red wine
1/2 cup pitted ripe olives
1/4 cup chopped parsley
salt and freshly ground pepper to taste
accompaniment: hot toast, English muffins
   or waffles

In the top pan (blazer) of a chafing dish placed directly over the flame, sauté the bacon until the fat is rendered. Add the livers to the pan and cook for 3 minutes, turning the livers frequently until browned. Add onion and bell pepper and cook 2 minutes. Add tarragon and wine and cook 5 minutes. Add olives, parsley, salt and pepper. Heat through and serve on hot toast, English muffins or waffles.

Variation Substitute sliced lamb or veal kidneys for chicken livers.

VEAL KIDNEYS, FLAMBÉED

Serves 4
3 tablespoons butter
4 veal kidneys, cut into 1/4-inch-thick slices
1 cup sliced mushrooms
2 shallots, minced
1/3 cup brandy, warmed
1/2 teaspoon dry mustard
salt and freshly ground pepper to taste
1 cup heavy cream
garnish: 2 tablespoons chopped parsley
accompaniment: freshly made toast or patty shells

In the top pan (blazer) of a chafing dish placed directly over the flame, melt the butter and sauté the kidneys, mushrooms and shallots over a brisk fire for 5 minutes or until kidneys are brown. Add the warmed brandy and ignite; when the flame burns out, add the mustard, salt, pepper and cream and heat through. Garnish with parsley and serve immediately over toast or in patty shells.

TABLETOP COOKERY

CREAMED TURKEY AND MUSHROOMS

Serves 4
1 cup sliced mushrooms
2 tablespoons chopped onion
2 tablespoons butter
1 tablespoon flour
1 cup half-and-half
2 eggs, beaten
1/4 cup Madeira or sherry
2 cups diced cooked turkey
2 tablespoons chopped parsley
pinch of freshly grated nutmeg
salt and freshly ground pepper to taste
accompaniments:
    hot buttered toast or freshly cooked rice
    slivered toasted almonds

In the top pan (blazer) of a chafing dish placed directly over the flame, sauté the mushrooms and onion in butter for 3 minutes; add the flour and cook and stir 1 minute. Gradually add half-and-half and continue stirring until smooth and thickened. Place the top pan over the hot water pan (lower pan). Blend 1/2 cup of the hot mixture with the beaten eggs and return to the pan. Continue to cook, stirring constantly, for 2 minutes. Add Madeira, turkey, parsley, nutmeg, salt and pepper and heat through. Serve over toast or rice and top with almonds.

Variations
• Substitute 2 cups cooked flaked crab meat for turkey, adding it at the same time as Madeira.
• Substitute 2 7-ounce cans of tuna, drained, for turkey, adding it at the same time as Madeira; omit salt and add 1 cup fresh, cooked peas, if desired.

FONDUE DIPPING SAUCES

Curry Sauce
1/4 cup fresh lemon juice
1/2 teaspoon salt
1 teaspoon curry powder
pinch of cayenne pepper
1 egg
1 cup peanut or corn oil

Combine all ingredients except oil in a blender and blend for 10 seconds. Gradually add the oil and blend until thick and smooth.

Lemon Mayonnaise
1/4 cup fresh lemon juice
1 strip lemon peel
1 cup mayonnaise
1 green onion, cut up
1 clove garlic

Combine all ingredients in a blender and blend until smooth. Chill until ready to use.

Horseradish Sauce
1 cup (1/2 pint) sour cream
1 tablespoon prepared horseradish
1 teaspoon fresh lemon juice

Combine all ingredients in a blender and blend until smooth. Chill until ready to use.

Flavored Butters
Garlic butter Soften 1/4 pound butter and blend in 1 or 2 cloves garlic, minced.
Tarragon butter Soften 1/4 pound butter and blend in 1 tablespoon minced tarragon or 1 teaspoon dried tarragon.
Bleu cheese butter Soften 1/4 pound butter and blend in 1/4 cup crumbled bleu cheese.
Anchovy butter Soften 1/4 pound butter and blend in 2 anchovy fillets, mashed, or 2 tablespoons anchovy paste.

TABLETOP COOKERY

SWISS FONDUE

Serves 4 to 6
1 clove garlic
2 cups dry white wine
1-1/2 pounds imported Swiss or Gruyère cheese,
    grated or cut into small cubes
2 teaspoons cornstarch, mixed with
1/4 cup kirsch
pinch of freshly ground pepper
pinch of freshly grated nutmeg
French bread, cut into 1-inch cubes
accompaniments:
    green salad or fresh fruit for dessert
    a dry white wine, such as Riesling

Rub the inside of a fondue pot or blazer (top pan) of a chafing dish with the garlic clove, then discard garlic. Heat the wine in the pot placed over flame and add cheese, stirring constantly until smooth. When bubbles begin to appear, add the cornstarch and kirsch mixture. Season with pepper and nutmeg. Fondue should be kept slightly bubbling while cooking. Spear bread cubes with a fondue fork, roll in fondue and eat. Serve with a green salad or fresh fruit for dessert and white wine.

BEEF FONDUE

Serves 4 to 6
peanut or corn oil
2 pounds tender beef steak, such as fillet or sirloin,
    cut into 1-inch cubes
accompaniments:
    various condiments and sauces such as horse-
        radish, mustard, Tabasco, Curry Sauce,
        Lemon Mayonnaise, anchovy, garlic or bleu
        cheese butter, page 171
    French bread
    chopped onions, sliced tomatoes and pickles

Fill a fondue pot or chafing dish to no more than one-half full with oil. Place over flame and heat to 375° or until a cube of bread or meat sizzles upon contact with oil. Spear meat with fondue fork and cook to desired doneness in the oil. Transfer to another fork, dip in accompanying sauces and eat with remaining accompaniments. Do not eat from fondue fork as it may burn your mouth.

Variations A mixture of various meats and seafood may be used, such as lamb, veal, chicken breast, shrimp, scallops, oysters, salmon or swordfish.

BROTH FONDUE

Serves 4 to 6
3 cups chicken stock
1 cup dry white wine
1 tablespoon minced tarragon, or
1 teaspoon dried tarragon
1/4 cup minced green onions
1/4 teaspoon freshly ground pepper
2 pounds tender beef steak, such as fillet,
    London broil or sirloin, cut into 1-inch cubes
brandy (optional)
accompaniments:
    French bread
    various seasonings or sauces for dipping, such
        as mustard, catsup, horseradish, Worcester-
        shire sauce, Tabasco, pickles and onions

In a fondue pot, chafing dish or firepot, combine
all the ingredients except meat and brandy and
simmer for 15 minutes. Spear meat with fondue
fork and cook to desired doneness in broth. Serve
with accompaniments. When all meat has been
cooked, add a splash of brandy to stock, if desired,
and serve broth in individual cups.

Variations A mixture of various meats or seafood
may be used, such as chicken breast, lamb, shrimp,
scallops, oysters or firm fish fillets.

TABLETOP COOKERY

SHABU SHABU

Serves 6 to 8

2 pounds boneless lean tender steak, such as
  tenderloin, sirloin or rib, sliced 1/8 inch thick
1 pound Napa cabbage, leaves separated and
  halved if large
1 bunch spinach or watercress, tough stems
  removed
2 carrots, cut diagonally into thin slices
8 green onions, cut into 4-inch lengths
1 pound fresh bean-curd cakes, cut into
  1-inch cubes
1/2 pound button mushrooms
2 quarts chicken stock or dashi*
accompaniment: freshly cooked rice (optional)
assorted sauces and condiments:
  Lemon and Soy Sauce, following
  Sesame and Soy Sauce, following
  seeded and minced small dried red chili peppers
  grated ginger root
  minced green onions

Prepare meat and vegetables and arrange on large platters; place sauces and condiments in bowls. Surround cooking pot with the platters and bowls. Provide each diner with a plate, a rice bowl, a pair of chopsticks to hold the foods while they are cooking, small bowls for dipping sauces and soup bowls or cups. Place the stock in a firepot or the top pan (blazer) of a chafing dish placed directly over the flame. When stock is bubbling, each diner selects foods from the platters with his chopsticks and cooks them in the stock until they are done to his preference. The foods are then eaten with the sauces and condiments. When all cooking is done, serve broth in cups or bowls.

*Japanese soup stock; instant variety available in Japanese markets.

Lemon and Soy Sauce Combine equal parts Japanese soy sauce and fresh lemon juice.

Sesame and Soy Sauce Combine 1/2 cup toasted sesame seeds, ground, 1/4 cup each Japanese soy sauce and mirin (Japanese sweet rice wine) or sherry and 1 tablespoon sugar.

CHINESE FIREPOT

2 pounds any combination of boneless meats or
  seafood, cut in bite-sized pieces, such as chicken,
  beef, lamb, chicken livers, heart, kidney, shrimp,
  oysters, scallops, firm fresh fish fillets, clams,
  squid, abalone
2 pounds any combination of vegetables, such as:
  spinach, Napa cabbage, iceberg lettuce,
    watercress or other leafy vegetable, cut in
    manageable pieces or left whole if small
  bamboo shoots and water chestnuts, sliced
  fresh bean-curd cakes, cut into 1-inch cubes
  green onions and leeks, cut into 2-inch lengths
  snow peas
  cellophane noodles, soaked in warm water
    to soften and cut in half
2 quarts chicken stock
assorted sauces and condiments: soy sauce,
  oyster sauce*, hoisin sauce*, Oriental sesame
  oil*, toasted sesame seeds, minced ginger root,
  garlic, green onions and seeded small dried red
  chili peppers

Prepare meats, seafood and vegetables and arrange
on large platters; place sauces and condiments in
bowls. Surround cooking pot with the platters and
bowls. Provide each diner with a plate, a wire-mesh
ladle to hold the foods while they are cooking, a
pair of chopsticks, small bowls for mixing sauces
and a soup bowl and spoon for eating the broth
and noodles. Place the stock in a firepot or the top
pan (blazer) of a chafing dish placed directly over
the flame. When stock is bubbling, each diner
selects foods from the platters, places them in the
ladle and cooks them in the stock to desired doneness. The foods are then eaten with the sauces and
condiments. When all cooking is done, add noodles
to stock and cook until tender, about 3 minutes.
Serve noodles and broth in soup bowls

*Available in Oriental markets.

TABLETOP COOKERY

YOSENABE

Serves 6

1 pound boneless chicken breast meat, cut
   into 1/2-inch-thick slices
12 medium-sized shrimp, shelled and deveined
12 small fresh clams in the shell, well scrubbed
12 scallops
1/2 pound fresh spinach leaves
1/2 pound Napa cabbage, cut into 2-inch pieces
1 carrot, cut into thin diagonal slices
1 cup sliced bamboo shoots
4 to 6 green onions, cut into 3-inch lengths
1 ounce cellophane noodles, soaked in warm
   water to soften and cut in half

Dashi Sauce
1 quart dashi* or chicken stock
1/2 cup Japanese soy sauce
1/4 cup mirin (Japanese sweet rice wine) or sherry

accompaniment: freshly cooked rice

Put chicken, seafood, vegetables and noodles in a large skillet placed over a hibachi or in a Mongolian firepot. Combine ingredients for Dashi Sauce and pour over all. Cook for 20 minutes or until chicken is tender; vegetables should remain crisp. Serve in bowls and accompany with rice.

*Japanese soup stock; instant variety available in Japanese markets.

SUKIYAKI

Serves 4 to 6

1 pound boneless rib steak, sirloin or fillet, sliced
  paper-thin (freezing meat until slightly firm
  makes slicing easier)
1/2 cup sliced onions
4 to 6 green onions, cut into 1-1/2-inch lengths
1 cup sliced mushrooms
1 cup sliced bamboo shoots
1/2 pound fresh bean-curd cakes, cut into
  1-inch cubes
1 ounce cellophane noodles, soaked in warm
  water to soften
1/2 pound Napa cabbage or spinach leaves, cut
  into 2-inch pieces
1/4 cup minced beef suet or peanut oil

Sauce
1/2 cup Japanese soy sauce
1/2 cup dashi* or beef stock
1/4 cup mirin (Japanese sweet rice wine) or sherry
3 tablespoons sugar

accompaniment: freshly cooked rice

Arrange the meat and each vegetable artistically in its own pile on a platter. Combine sauce mixture and have ready at the table. Place a skillet over a hibachi and add the suet or oil to the pan. When hot, add half of meat, each vegetable, bean curd and noodles to pan, keeping each ingredient in its own pile. Pour half the sauce over all and cook until vegetables are just tender-crisp. As the suki-yaki is cooking, turn meat and vegetables occasionally to cook evenly. When done, remove from heat and serve from pan with individual bowls of rice. Repeat cooking with remaining ingredients.

*Japanese soup stock; instant variety available in Japanese markets.

TABLETOP COOKERY

OYAKO DOMBURI
(Chicken and Eggs with Rice)

Serves 4
1 pound boneless chicken breast meat, cut into
    bite-size pieces
1/4 cup Japanese soy sauce
1 tablespoon sugar
1 tablespoon sake or sherry
3 tablespoons peanut oil
1 cup sliced mushrooms
4 to 6 green onions, cut into 1-1/2-inch lengths
1/2 cup fresh peas (1/2 pound, unshelled)
1/2 cup dashi* or chicken stock
4 eggs, beaten
accompaniment: freshly cooked rice

Marinate the chicken pieces in the soy sauce, sugar and sake for 30 minutes. Drain, reserving marinade. Heat the oil in a skillet placed over a hibachi and stir-fry the chicken pieces for 5 minutes. Add the mushrooms, green onions, peas and stock. Cook 5 minutes more; then pour eggs over all and cook until eggs are set but moist. Serve over individual bowls of rice; drizzle reserved marinade over all.

*Japanese soup stock; instant variety available in Japanese markets.

JUHN KOL

any combination of:
    large prawns, shelled and deveined
    firm fresh fish fillets, cut into bite-sized pieces
    scallops or oysters
    chicken breasts, boned and cut into bite-sized
      pieces
    tender cuts of beef, lamb or pork, sliced in
      thin strips
    vegetables such as button mushrooms, scallion
      bulbs, eggplant, zucchini and sweet red or
      green peppers, cut into 1-inch pieces

**Marinade (for 1 pound of meat and 1 pound of
    vegetables)**
3/4 cup Japanese soy sauce or thin Chinese
    soy sauce
3 tablespoons peanut oil
1 teaspoon Oriental sesame oil*
1/4 cup ground toasted sesame seeds**
1/4 cup sugar
1/2 teaspoon ground small dried red chili peppers
1/2 cup chopped green onions
2 cloves garlic, minced
1 teaspoon minced ginger root

accompaniment: freshly cooked rice

Combine marinade ingredients and marinate meats and vegetables for at least 2 hours. Drain, reserving marinade. Skewer meats and vegetables separately. Let each person grill his own at the table on a hibachi, basting with marinade. Serve with marinade for dipping and accompany with rice.

Note Plan on 1/3 pound each of meat and vegetables per person.

*Available in Oriental markets.

**Place sesame seeds on a dry skillet over low heat and stir constantly until golden. Remove from heat; let cool and pulverize to a powder in a blender or use a mortar and pestle.

TABLETOP COOKERY

TERIYAKI MARINADE

1 cup Japanese soy sauce
2 tablespoons mirin (Japanese sweet rice wine)
  or sherry
1 teaspoon grated ginger root
2 tablespoons peanut oil

Combine all ingredients and use as marinade in the following recipes.

BEEF TERIYAKI

Serves 4 to 6
Marinate 2 pounds tender beef steak, such as tenderloin, sirloin, skirt or rib steak, in Teriyaki Marinade for 20 minutes. Drain, reserving marinade, and grill over hot charcoal to desired doneness, turning once. Place on heated platter, slice thinly, pour remaining marinade over meat and serve with freshly cooked rice and sliced tomatoes and watercress sprigs.

FISH TERIYAKI

Serves 4 to 6
Marinate 2 pounds fresh fish fillets such as sea bass, halibut or ling cod, cut 1 inch thick, in Teriyaki Marinade for 1 hour. Drain, reserving marinade, and grill over hot charcoal about 5 minutes on each side. Serve with freshly cooked rice, remaining marinade and a spinach salad.

TERIYAKI BURGERS

Serves 6
Combine 1/3 cup Teriyaki Marinade with 2 pounds lean ground beef. Form into 6 thick patties and grill over hot charcoal to desired doneness, turning once. Serve with remaining marinade and sliced tomatoes and onions on toasted buns or with freshly cooked rice.

CHICKEN TERIYAKI

Serves 4 to 6
Cut a 3-pound fryer chicken into serving pieces (or use 3 pounds chicken parts) and marinate in Teriyaki Marinade for 2 hours. Drain, reserving marinade, and grill over hot charcoal 15 minutes or until done, turning occasionally. Serve with freshly cooked rice, remaining marinade and Grilled Japanese Eggplant, following.

Grilled Japanese Eggplant
Place whole, small Japanese eggplant over hot charcoal and grill, turning frequently, until centers are soft to the touch, about 15 minutes. Serve the eggplant with some of the marinade.

TABLETOP COOKERY

BROILED SALMON

Serves 4 to 6
2 pounds salmon fillets, cut 1 inch thick
1/3 cup fresh lemon juice
2 tablespoons flour
salt and freshly ground pepper to taste
accompaniment:
  Broiled Potatoes, following
  green salad

Marinate salmon in lemon juice for 1 hour. Dust fillets with flour, salt and pepper. Grill over hot charcoal, about 5 minutes on each side.

Broiled Potatoes
Boil small new potatoes about 6 minutes, or until just tender. Dip in melted butter and broil over hot charcoal until brown and crispy, turning frequently. Serve with additional butter and sprinkle with chopped chives, parsley or dill.

GRILLED SWEETBREADS

Serves 6
2 pounds sweetbreads
2 tablespoons vinegar
3 slices bacon, cut into 1-inch pieces
4 tablespoons butter
1 tablespoon fresh lemon juice
1/4 teaspoon dried tarragon
6 slices freshly made toast
accompaniments:
  tomato wedges
  watercress sprigs

Parboil sweetbreads in water to cover with the vinegar for 5 minutes; drain. Remove and discard excess fat and membranes. Cut sweetbreads in 1/2-inch-thick slices. Thread on skewers alternating with bacon and grill over hot charcoal 10 minutes, turning frequently. Cream butter, lemon juice and tarragon together and spread on toast. Serve grilled sweetbreads on toast with accompaniments.

MONGOLIAN LAMB ON SKEWERS

Serves 4 to 6
2 pounds boneless leg of lamb,
   cut into 1-inch cubes
1 onion, cut into 1-inch chunks
1 bell pepper, cut into 1-inch chunks
toasted sesame seeds

Marinade
2 tablespoons hoisin sauce*
2 tablespoons soy sauce
2 tablespoons dry sherry
2 tablespoons peanut oil
1 tablespoon sugar
1/4 teaspoon five-spice powder
pinch of cayenne pepper

accompaniments:
   freshly cooked rice
   fresh pineapple and mango slices

Combine marinade ingredients and marinate lamb for 2 hours. Skewer meat alternately with pieces of onion and bell pepper. Grill over hot charcoal about 10 minutes, turning frequently and basting with any remaining marinade. Sprinkle with sesame seeds just before serving. Serve with rice and fresh pineapple and mango slices.

*Available in Oriental markets.

LAMB KEBOBS

Serves 4 to 6
2 pounds boneless lamb, preferably from leg,
   cut into 1-inch cubes
1/3 cup fresh lemon juice
1/2 teaspoon dried rosemary
2 cloves garlic, minced
2 tablespoons olive oil
salt and freshly ground pepper to taste
1 onion, cut into 1-inch pieces
1 bell pepper, cut into 1-inch pieces
2 firm ripe tomatoes, cut into wedges
accompaniment: freshly cooked rice, pilaf or
   bulgur

Marinate the lamb in a mixture of the lemon juice, rosemary, garlic, olive oil and salt and pepper for 20 minutes. Thread meat on skewers alternately with onion, bell pepper and tomato and grill over hot charcoal for 10 minutes, turning and basting occasionally. Serve with rice, pilaf or bulgur.

TABLETOP COOKERY

GRILLED CHICKEN LIVERS AND BACON

Serves 4 to 6
1-1/2 pounds chicken livers, halved or cut in thirds
6 slices bacon, cut into 1-1/2-inch pieces

Marinade
1/4 cup soy sauce
2 tablespoons sherry
1/2 teaspoon curry powder
1 teaspoon grated ginger root
1/4 cup finely minced green onions
1 tablespoon peanut oil

accompaniments:
    freshly cooked rice or bulgur
    Grilled Zucchini, following

Combine marinade ingredients and marinate chicken livers in this mixture 1 hour. Drain well, reserving any marinade, and skewer livers alternately with bacon pieces. Grill over hot charcoal until bacon is crisp, turning frequently and basting with remaining marinade. Serve with rice or bulgur and Grilled Zucchini.

Grilled Zucchini
Cut small zucchini in half lengthwise and brush with peanut oil seasoned to taste with minced garlic, salt and freshly ground pepper. Grill over hot coals, about 8 minutes on each side.

| Soup Pot | Dutch Oven | Slow Cooker | Pressure Cooker | Wet Clay Cooker | Roasting Pan | Flameproof Casserole |

| Pie Pan | Baking Dish | Soufflé Dish | Skillet | Wok | Chafing Dish | Fondue Pot | Hibachi |

INDEX

INDEX

INDEX

INDEX

MARGARET GIN

Margaret Gin is well known to 101 cookbook collectors from her previously published works: *Regional Cooking of China, Country Cookery from Many Lands,* and *Innards and Other Variety Meats.* Mrs. Gin's Chinese ancestry, her girlhood in the southwestern United States, her travels to Europe and the many years she has resided in San Francisco have given her a broad insight into the many ethnic cuisines whose recipes comprise this book. Between testing recipes and writing cookbooks, raising two teen-age sons, and entertaining frequently with her husband William in their homes in San Francisco and Napa Valley, multi-talented Margaret Gin works as a free-lance ski wear and fashion designer.

RIK OLSON

An artist versatile in many media, Rik Olson completed the drawings for this book after spending eight years in Europe as an arts and crafts instructor for the United States Army. While he was abroad, his graphics and photographs were widely exhibited in Germany and Italy, winning a number of awards in Frankfurt and Florence. A native Californian, Rik Olson received his BFA degree from California College of Arts and Crafts and later studied photography in Germany and etching in Florence. He and his wife presently live in San Francisco.